CLASSIC
JETLINERS

CLASSIC
JETLINERS

OSPREY
AEROSPACE

First published in Great Britain in 1994
by Osprey, an imprint of Reed Consumer
Books Limited
Michelin House, 81 Fulham Road,
London SW3 6RB
and Auckland, Melbourne, Singapore
and Toronto

ISBN 1 855324040

Edited by Tony Holmes
Page design by Paul Kime
Printed and bound in Hong Kong
Produced by Mandarin Offset

Front cover The rare sight of a
Boeing 707-328C on final approach
to London Heathrow is captured by
the camera as Cyprus-registered 5B-
DAZ nears runway 27L in August
1993. This aircraft entered service
with Air France as 'Chateau de
Lude' in June 1967, and more than
a quarter of century later was still
paying its way by hauling cargo
for Avistar

Back cover Having been
prematurely retired from service in
favour of more Boeing 737/757s,
three of British Airways' grounded
fleet of two-dozen Trident 3Bs,
inherited from British European
Airways (BEA) in the mid 1970s, sit
silently on a forgotten part of the
ramp at Heathrow in spring 1986

Title page The weather-beaten nose
of a veteran Trans Mediterranean
Airways (TMA) 707-321C homes in
on London Heathrow during a
warm afternoon in July 1989. Ice,
hail and rain have battered away the
paint from the radome and the
fuselage skin aft of the cockpit
windows, making this workhorse
look a little the worse for wear.
Clearly seen clustered near the line
dividing the bare aluminium from
the green TMA livery are the
aircraft's air data and airspeed
indicator probes, as well as the stall
warning indicator

For a catalogue of all books published by Osprey Aerospace
please write to:

**The Marketing Department, Reed Consumer Books,
1st Floor, Michelin House, 81 Fulham Road, London SW3 6RB**

Above Just as the cargo business has perpetuated the life of older 707s, DC-8s and DC-9s, so it has also kept alive a huge fleet of 727s. Here, two Federal Express 727 freighters simmer in the dry heat of an Arizona afternoon in April 1993. The aircraft wait on the cargo ramp at Phoenix Sky Harbour airport for the hectic evening rush to begin when they will be loaded up with packages and parcels and despatched to FedEx's hub in Nashville, Tennessee. The two trijets also represent the full span of almost 20 years of 727 production at Renton. 'Jeremy David', the 727-2S2F nearest to the camera, was one of the last 727s built, its first flight taking place in April 1984, whilst N511FE is a 28-year old veteran dating from 1965. The older aircraft, a short bodied 727-25, was originally built for Eastern Airlines, where it served until the collapse of the carrier in 1989. It was converted to freighter configuration for FedEx the same year. Boeing initially forecast sales of around 300 727s, but they ended up building no less than 1831, with 'Jeremy David' and its cohorts being amongst the last trijets pushed out of the Renton factory in 1984

Introduction

The ear-shattering roar of jet engines, and the trail of exhaust smoke left in their wake, are classic hallmarks of the first jetliners. The awesome sights and sounds of these pioneer aircraft thrilled a new generation of passengers as turbine technology ushered in a golden era of globe-shrinking air travel.

The stunning photographs in this book help capture the essence of that lost age. Vivid images from airports around the world conjure up an atmosphere permeated with the smell of jet fuel and the shrill whine of the early turbofans and turbojets. Unfortunately, the hallmarks captured so well by the lens, also spell the doom of these geriatric jets.

Time is running out for the last survivors of the jet revolution because of new environmental standards on noise and exhaust emissions. These will be imposed by the year 2000, and it foreshadows the end for most early jets still scratching a living in the skies of Europe, North America and the Asia-Pacific region.

The disappearance of the first jetliners will be celebrated by many and mourned by few. After all, they are generally thought of as inefficient, gas-guzzling, noisy, hard to maintain and expensive to operate. Yet, suprisingly, some of these dinosaurs have carved themselves a niche in the marketplace from which it is hard to prise them. The McDonnell Douglas DC-8, for example, is a favourite aircraft for many US air cargo and express parcel operators. Out of a current world fleet of around 170, some 110 are based in the US.

Conversely, many of the economically hard-pressed airlines of Central and South America, Africa and parts of the Middle East, are attracted by the cheap purchasing and leasing costs of aircraft such as the Boeing 707. Out of a current world fleet of around 180 commercial 707s, over 130 are flown by operators in those parts of the world.

Some of the lucky ones could also see a stay of execution because of the economic recession of the 1990s. Although the same recession grounded many jets for good, it also forced some airlines to cancel orders for modern types and think of ways to keep the old ones going. Hushkits, which reduce the noise made by an engine, are being developed for several types. In some cases, such as the McDonnell Douglas DC-9 and Boeing 727, the original engines may even be replaced with new technology powerplants.

In all, some 1900 'old' jets are expected to retire before the end of the century. This high level of 'jetocide' means this collection of photographs will fast become a valuable record of a vanishing world.

Right Vintage Douglas piston-engined transports form a fitting frame for some classic jet freighters lined up at Miami in 1990. Centre stage is DC-8-55F N29549, originally delivered in 1965 to Trans Caribbean Airways as N8785R 'James Roy II', and pictured in the colours of Costa Rican-based cargo operator LACSA Carga. The aircraft was bought by American International Airways in 1992. The distinctive Pratt & Whitney engine installation of the -50 series is well illustrated in this shot. The number one engine, closest to the camera, clearly shows the separate cold air cascade thrust reverser midway along the nacelle. The JT3D-3 engine also has an ejector and clamshell reverser at the main exhaust to redirect hot gases forward

Contents

Boeing 707

Left Mid-day sunshine glints off the polished aluminium rudder of Florida West Boeing 707-351C N740FW as it is towed across the Miami International ramp in March 1988. Florida West operates a fleet of 707s from its Miami base on scheduled and charter freight operations to Bogota, Buenos Aires, Panama City Managua and other cities in Central and South America. Charter operations occasionally take the aircraft as far afield as Europe and the Middle East. N740FW first flew in November 1966 and was delivered the following month to Northwest Orient Airlines where it served faithfully until 1974. Northwest originally ordered the Douglas DC-8 but discovered that the first models on order could not meet some key long range requirements such as their Seattle to Tokyo route. For some time the airline used the long range 720B, a shortened variant of the 707, but later purchased the longer range 707-320 Intercontinental as load factors grew. After Northwest, N740FW served with Jugoslovenski Aerotransport (JAT) and Nigeria Airways before being bought by Florida West in 1987

Above N740FW pictured three years earlier in service with Jugoslovenski Aerotransport. Here, the 707-351C, registered YU-AGJ, is just commencing its take-off roll from runway 27 Left at London Heathrow

Right MEA Boeing 707-323C OD-AHD rests at London Heathrow on an autumn day in 1985. MEA's stalwart fleet of 707s have been the backbone of its services throughout the troubled times from its Beirut base. Some of the fleet have been lost to artillery and missile attacks during more than 20 years of war, their carcases being used to supply spares for the survivors. Noticeable in this view of the aircraft is the distinctive difference between the two pylons carrying the Pratt & Whitney JT3D

turbofans. The port outer engine (number one) lacks the small inlet above the main intake which is situated above the number two, three and four engines on most models of the 707. The inlet feeds air to a turbocompressor which compresses it for use in air-conditioning packs buried in the wing root. The air is then cooled or heated, as appropriate, before being ducted into the cabin. This particular aircraft began service as an American Airlines 'Astrojet' in August 1967, eventually joining MEA in November 1982

BOEING 707-320B AND -320C

Type: long-range passenger and (320C) cargo or passenger/cargo transport
Span: 44.42 m (145 ft 9 in)
Length: 46.61 m (152 ft 11 in)
Height: 12.93 m (42 ft 5 in)
Wing area: 279.64 m² (3010 sq ft)
Weight: maximum 151,315 kg (333,600 lb); empty 63,740 kg (140,524 lb); (320C) all-cargo 60,725 kg (133,874 lb)
Powerplant: four 8165-kg (18,000-lb) st Pratt & Whitney JT3D-3 or -3B two-shaft turbofans, or 8618-kg (19,000-lb) JT3D-7s
Performance: maximum cruising speed 966 km/h (600 mph); economical cruising speed 886 km/h (550 mph); range with maximum payload 9915 km (6160 miles)
Payload: 24,709 kg (54,476 lb); (320C) all-cargo 43,603 kg (96,126 lb); seats for 189 passengers or, with two extra emergency exits, 202
Crew: four
Production: 188; (320C) 336

Right With noise being one of the biggest, if not the main, enemy of the 707, some operators have taken steps to prolong their investments by hushkitting their aircraft. One of these is MEA, who have opted for the 'Super Q' conversion offered by Comtran International of the USA. Here Boeing 707-3B4C OD-AFD comes over the runway approach lighting at London Heathrow in January 1991. Other than the huge red lettering pronouncing Foxtrot Delta to be a 'New Q', the only external clue to the conversion is the extended engine intake and fan exhaust ducts which primarily 'hush' the fan and compressor noise. The kit includes liners made by Rohr Industries DynaRohr. The low angled light of the January evening highlights the enlarged bypass duct collar passing around the 'chest' of each engine. The kit improves the aircraft to Stage 2 standards by reducing the standard 707 100 EPNdB (environmentally perceived noise decibel) footprint from 5.6 nm (10.4 km) to 2.8 nm (5.2 km) without affecting capabilities such as anti-icing and thrust reversal. This aircraft is also unusual in that it is still flying for its original owner. In this case, the 707 was delivered in October 1969, and having served briefly on lease with Saudia Arabian Airlines and Nigeria Airways, returned full-time to MEA for further service

Above Black exhaust trails betray climb-out power as TMA Boeing 707-321C soars out of London Heathrow in October 1991. Three thousand pounds of hydraulic pressure have been used to retract the undercarriage and aerodynamically clean-up the aircraft as it accelerates towards a climb-out speed of 200 kts (230 mph) – flaps are still set at the 17° take-off position. TMA cargo 707 OD-AGP was photographed en-route to its home base at Beirut, Lebanon, from where it operates scheduled cargo services linking Europe, the Middle-East, South East Asia, the Far East and the USA. This particular aircraft first flew from Boeing's Renton production site on 14 June 1967 (on the very same day the editor was born!) and was delivered to Pan American World Airways eight days later as 'Clipper Golden Fleece'. TMA acquired the 707 in June 1977

Above right The bright yellow tail of a Sudan Airways Boeing 707-3J8C stands out against the gloom of a June day at London Heathrow in 1986. A British Midland McDonnell Douglas DC-9 hurries along a taxyway in the middle distance. One of the last 707s built for airline use, ST-AFB made its maiden flight 12 years to the month before this photograph was taken. Most of the 707s manufactured after 'Foxtrot Bravo' were military or government transport versions for nations such as Iran and Saudi Arabia. The majority of the last 90 aircraft, made from 1977 to the last delivery in 1992, were platforms for the airborne warning and control system (AWACS) E-3 variant, which sports a distinctive radar dish above the aft fuselage

Right Air Seychelles Boeing 707-324C S7-2HM is pushed back in bright sunshine at Zurich airport at the start of its long journey to its temporary home in the Indian Ocean. The aircraft was almost 20 years old when captured on film in October 1988, and had seen service with Continental Airlines in the USA and Varig in Brazil, before beginning a long career with various leasing companies. Air Seychelles returned S7-2HM to Equator Leasing Incorporated one year later, and the aircraft was then picked up by Angola Air Charter in July 1991

BOEING 707-320

Type: long-range passenger and cargo transport
Span: 43.41 m (142 ft 5 in)
Length: 46.61 m (152 ft 11 in)
Height: 12.7 m (41 ft 8 in)
Wing area: 268.68 m² (2892 sq ft)
Weight: maximum 141,520 kg (312,000 lb); empty 61,235 kg (135,000 lb)
Powerplant: four 7167-kg (15,800-lb) st Pratt & Whitney JT4A-3 two-shaft turbojets; later re-engined with 7620-kg (16,800-lb) JT4A-9s and finally 7495-kg (17,500-lb) JT4A-11s
Performance: maximum cruising speed 969 km/h (602 mph); economical cruising speed 876 km/h (545 mph); range with maximum payload 7700 km (4784 miles)
Payload: 24,950 kg (55,000 lb); seats for up to 189 passengers
Crew: four
Production: 69

Above Boeing 707-328C 'Suez' of Zarkani Aviation Services (ZAS) Airline of Egypt awaits maintenance at Stansted Airport under a brooding September sky in 1985. While the task of keeping an old 707 flying can be a financial headache, the relatively low purchase price of the aircraft has made it a viable option for airlines from developing nations. SU-DAB was formerly known as 'Chateau de Lude' when it began service with Air France as a new 707 in June 1967. It became 'Suez' when bought by ZAS in March 1983. The aircraft later passed through several leasing agencies before ending up with Avistar as 5B-DAZ – this jet is also featured on the cover of this volume

Above A Nigeria Airways Boeing 707-3F9C stands idle at Manston in Kent in October 1993, some nine months after having been repossessed by a finance company. The aircraft has been out of service for so long that it will need to have a C Check, or annual maintenance review, before being cleared for flying once again. The airframe, which is still in good condition nonetheless, has been maintained by Aer Lingus for Nigeria Airways since 1988, and is one of the 'youngest' 707s around with only 30,700 flying hours 'on the clock', as well as 11,400 landing and take-off cycles. It was originally delivered directly to the African carrier from Boeing in January 1973

Above and left In a hangar not far from the Nigerian 707, a well-used veteran sister aircraft belonging to DAS (Dairo Air Service) Air Cargo receives its C Check from Jet Support at Manston. This high-time 707-338C has clocked up 80,000 flight hours and 25,000 cycles since it was first delivered to QANTAS in February 1965. In service with DAS Air Cargo since 1984, it regularly plies scheduled routes from Nairobi, Lagos and Entebbe to London Gatwick. Irregular flights are also made from Nairobi to Amsterdam with cargoes of flowers

Above Fatigue and corrosion problems are constant enemies of classic jetliners. Air Gambia 707-323B HR-AMW receives undivided attention for a cracked front (main) wing spar from the Manston-based Jet Support Centre in October 1993. The work was completed in three weeks and the aircraft returned to service flying from Banjul to London Gatwick

Above Lowa Limited owned Boeing 707-330B N88ZL lines up for take-off on London Heathrow's runway 09 Right in March 1993. Spring sunshine highlights the front fan and intake area of the starboard Pratt & Whitney JT3D engines as they prepare to spool up to 18,000 lbs take-off thrust. Also picked out well are auxiliary air inlet doors around the fan casing, which are fully open to feed additional air to the engine during take-off and climb out. The spring loaded doors are closed during the cruise to reduce drag. This aircraft first flew at Renton on 7 December 1965, and was delivered to Lufthansa as 'Hannover' D-ABUF three weeks later. After a brief spell with Condor, the wholly owned charter subsidiary of Lufthansa, the 707 was retired by the German group in February 1981. US-based Lowa leased the aircraft from Aerommer Limited in 1984, this arrangement still existing a decade later

BOEING 720B

Type: short/medium-range passenger transport
Span: 39.87 m (130 ft 10 in)
Length: 41.68 m (136 ft 9 in)
Height: 12.67 m (41 ft 7 in)
Wing area: 234.2 m² (2521 sq ft)
Weight: maximum 106,140 kg (234,000 lb): empty 62,163 kg (115,000 lb)
Powerplant: four 8165-kg (18,000-lb) st Pratt & Whitney JT3D-3 turbofans (some still flying with 7718-kg (17,000-lb JT3D-1s)
Performance: maximum cruising speed 978 km/h (608 mph); economical cruising speed 858 km/h (533 mph); range with maximum payload 6614 km (4110 miles)
Payload: 18,600 kg (41,000 lbs); seats for up to 181 passengers
Crew: four
Production: 154

Left Geriatric jet hulks are an increasingly familiar sight around the world. Engineless, and with paint fading, this forlorn Boeing 720-059B awaits the cutter's torch at Miami in March 1988, almost five years after being withdrawn from use by Leaseway International. Registered as N4451B at the time of its demise, the 720 was originally built in 1961 for Columbian flag carrier Avianca. Sporting the name 'Bolivar', which was later changed to 'Cordova', the 720 served firstly with Avianca until July 1983 and then Monarch Aviation, followed soon after by Jet Star Incorporated. Leaseway purchased the airliner in November 1983 and then promptly grounded it that same month. The 720 was 16 ft 2 in shorter than the 707-320 and had a gross weight 35,000 lbs lighter than the longer range jet

Above The wings of this 707-344B arch up, relieved of the load of their Pratt & Whitney JT3D turbofans. This Guyana Airways aircraft, originally delivered to South African Airways in 1965, had been parked at Manston, England for four months when this shot was taken in late 1993. The 707 wing is renowned for its strength. In December 1965, a TWA 707 collided at 11,000 ft with an Eastern Airlines Lockheed Constellation over New York. More than 35 ft of the 707's left wing was torn off but the jet made it safely back to John F Kennedy airport, where it landed 19 minutes after the collision. This incident followed an earlier one in 1965 when a Pan Am 707 lost 25 ft of one wing after a jet engine exploded shortly after take-off from San Francisco. The aircraft landed safely at a miltary air base across the bay. Both incidents led to the apocryphal TWA maintenance telex: 'Amendment To Inoperative Equipment List – Effective immediately all Boeing 707s may be dispatched with right or left wing missing'

Above Heat shimmers on a Miami International airport taxyway as Boeing 707-331C CC-CAF crawls along under the intense Florida sunshine in April 1988. The Chilean-owned 707 plied cargo routes linking Santiago with Bogota, Frankfurt, Miami, New York, Panama City and Sao Paulo up until it was bought by Aerolineas Uruguayas in 1990. The aircraft was originally delivered to TWA as N5774T in October 1967, where it served as a 'Star Stream 707' for the US airline until 1978 when it was sold to Fast Air Carrier of Santiago

Right Most commercially operated 707s in the late 1980s and early 1990s owed their livelihood to the cargo business, this veteran Boeing 707-327C freighter being photographed between flights at Miami in March 1989. Originally delivered to Braniff Airways in October 1967 as N7103, the 707 passed through a succession of owners, including Singapore Airlines and Shanghai Airlines, before ending up with Ladeco Chilean Airlines in December 1988

Above One of the last European airlines to operate the 707 on regular passenger services was Air Portugal (TAP). Here, the carrier's Boeing 707-373C CS-TBJ is seen seconds away from touchdown on runway 27 Left at London Heathrow in August 1987. In this configuration the aircraft has been descending at 700 ft per minute with its leading-edge flaps deployed and full 50° landing flap selected for the last few moments of final approach. The TAP 707 is being slowed to around 138 kts before touchdown. Four months after this photograph was taken TAP sold the jet to Sicotra Aviation, who re-registered it as 9Q-CSB. The aircraft was originally delivered at the end of May 1966 to World Airways as N372WA

Above Bolivian-owned Boeing 707-323C CP-1698 swallows a freight pallet through its 7.5 ft by 11 ft cargo door at Miami International on a cloudless March day in 1988. This aircraft, originally delivered to American Airlines in February 1968 as N8406, will take up to 5693 cu ft of containerised cargo or freight pallets. A complete palletised cargo of 90,000 lbs can be loaded and unloaded in less than one hour

Right The same aircraft, the same airport, but one year later. Still flying cargo, Lloyd Aero Boliviano (LAB) Boeing 707-323C waits for yet another load. The 'C Jets', as Boeing called them, retained all the major features of the -320B Intercontinental, but had a beefed-up main deck and undercarriage to allow for heavier loading. 'C' could stand for convertible or combi as well as cargo. In the latter configuration it could be used simultaneously for both freight and passengers, with cargo pallets stored in the forward main deck area. The upper main deck provides 8000 cu ft of space and the two lower decks give a total of 1712 cu ft. Some of the space in the compartment below decks could also be used to store the 707's own cargo handling equipment, if necessary

Above left Pictured in the twilight of its career, Dominicana Boeing 707-399C HI-442 stands idle on the ramp at Miami in 1988 with its engine covers on. 'Puerto Plata' began service as 'County of Ayr' when it was delivered to Caledonian Airways shortly after Christmas 1967. After a short spell with British Overseas Airways Corporation (BOAC) in 1969, the aircraft re-joined the now re-named British Caledonian, following Caledonian's merger with British United Airways in November 1970. The 707 then spent seven years with Portuguese carrier TAP and a brief spell on lease to Nigeria Airways, before being retired in 1980. Dominica bought the aircraft in 1983 and operated it for several years before withdrawing it from use and storing it at Santo Domingo

Left High rise apartment complexes rise above Transcorp Boeing 707-330C and the hemmed-in apron of Hong Kong's Kai Tak airport in November 1986. With such evident overcrowding it is obvious why a new airport, Chek Lap Kok, is being constructed on the site of a small island close to the territory. As airport traffic has mushroomed in Asia, so has the demand for cargo capacity. In many cases the 707 was too small to meet the demand and has been replaced on trunk routes with widebody freighters. Originally delivered in November 1965 to Lufthansa as D-ABUA 'Europa', this aircraft retired after 20 years service with the German airline and was bought in 1985 by Transcorp Airways and named 'Perth'. Later re-named 'Hong Kong Kowloon Trader', the 707 then changed hands in November 1988 when it was bought by Ansett Air Freight. After flying for almost two years as 'Brisbane' it was withdrawn and stored at Perth airport. However, in December 1992 it was bought by Global Air and obtained a new lease of life as LZ-PVA

Above Iraqi Airways Boeing 707-370C YI-AGG is towed across the ramp in happier times at Beijing airport, China, in October 1986, having completed its journey from Baghdad. This aircraft was one of the last commercial 707s built and was delivered to the airline in October 1974. Although Iraq managed to save much of the airline's equipment from destruction by coalition forces during the 1991 Gulf War by ferrying it to India and Iran, the fleet is now largely idle. This is due to surrender terms imposed by the United Nations which prohibit all cross-border flights. As late as 1993 only internal flights by Antonov An-24s were permitted

Above Kuwait Airways Boeing 707-327C approaches London Heathrow on a clear March day in 1993. After the end of hostilities following the 1991 war with Iraq, Kuwait was faced with a mammoth re-building task. This also included the national airline which had seen its fleet of Airbus A300s, Boeing 767s and a 727 seized by Iraq. Those not destroyed, or that escaped capture by being abroad at the time of the Iraqi invasion, have been returned but in 1993 the airline was still depleted. Amongst the aircraft it leased was 707 OD-AGX, which came from TMA for cargo services. The aircraft was originally delivered to Braniff Airways in May 1966 and passed into full-time TMA ownership in 1980 after several years of operations under lease

Above and right Another aircraft that was pressed into service with Kuwait Airways was this Ghanian-registered 707 owned by Peak Aviation of the UK. The aircraft's engines are receiving close inspection during the 707's B-Check at the Jet Support Centre at Manston. The B-Check occurs every 120 days and normally keeps the 707 on the ground for around five days. After servicing the aircraft returned to freight duty between Kuwait, London Heathrow and Amsterdam on sub-lease to TMA Lebanon. The Pratt & Whitney JT3D engine was the major powerplant for the 707, and helped provide the springboard for P&W to launch the JT8D – the most successful jet engine in history. Most variants of the 707, including the Intercontinental 320B and 320C, used the JT3D-3 but some such as the basic -320 Intercontinental used the JT4A engine. Until the later -3 engines became available, the -4A was briefly the most powerful option for the 707, giving more than 2000 lbs thrust per engine more than the 13,500-lb thrust JT3C engine, which powered the first production -120 model 707s. Rolls-Royce had limited sales success with the Conway Mk 508-powered 707, which was dubbed the -420. The leading customer was BOAC, but sales were also made to Air India, Lufthansa, Varig and El Al. Rumour has it that Boeing's sales people were not too impressed when the first 707-420 for BOAC was painted with the identifying insignia 'Rolls-Royce 707'!

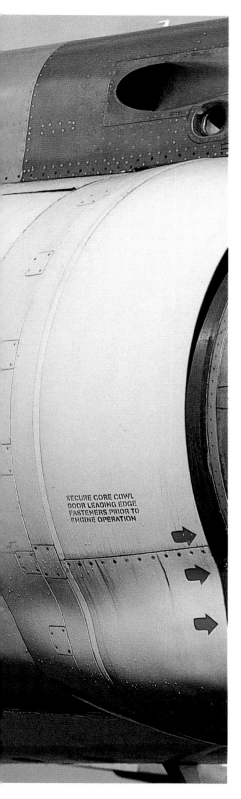

SECURE CORE COWL
DOOR LEADING EDGE
FASTENERS PRIOR TO
ENGINE OPERATION

Above Air Zimbabwe Boeing 707-330B Z-WKU coasts into London Gatwick from Amsterdam, where it stopped after an overnight flight from Harare. This is another former Lufthansa machine dating from January 1966 when it was delivered to the German airline as 'Dortmund'. Originally registered with Air Zimbabwe as VP-WKU when the African airline bought it in April 1982, the aircraft assumed its current identity when the country changed its register in 1983. The bright sunshine highlights the 707's distinctive high frequency communications antenna, occasionally mistaken for an air-speed indicator probe, mounted on top of the tail

Left The enlarged fan bypass duct collar of the Comtram International hushkit bulges out towards the right hand side of the picture in this view of an Air Gambia 707 at Manston. Comtram is moving all its hushkit installation work from California to San Antonio, Texas, where it is developing an even quieter Stage 3 kit for 707s with Quiet Nacelle and Aviation Leasing

Above Well travelled Kenya Airways Boeing 707-351B taxies at London Heathrow in unseasonal English June weather in 1986. This 707, 5Y-BBI, first flew in March 1968 and was delivered within three days of its maiden flight to Northwest Orient Airlines as N378US. It was bought by Kenya Airways in September 1977, and like sister aircraft 5Y-BBJ, 'Bravo India' was often used to transport Kenya's President Daniel Arap Moi until the arrival of the airline's Airbus A310s. In the background, sharing the overcast, is Oman Government-owned Vickers VC10 Srs 1103 A40-AB and a 707 belonging to fellow African carrier Nigeria Airways. A40-AB is now preserved at Brooklands, near Weybridge in the UK

Right These identical looking 707s normally face each other across the Atlantic Ocean from their respective bases in Guyana, South America and Gambia, Africa. The homes of most working 707s are found in Africa, South and Central America and the Middle East. In late 1993, more than 130 707s and a few 720s were still active in these regions, compared to 24 in the US, 13 in Europe and just six in the Asia-Pacific zone. The aircraft on the left, EL-AJT of Guyana Airways, had been stored for four months at Manston by the time this photograph was taken in late 1993. On the right, poking its distinctive Boeing snout into the shot is Air Gambia 707 HR-AMW. The operators of the latter jet ceased operations in January 1994 after declaring themselves bankrupt

Right and opposite The heavy reliance on electro-mechanical instruments, well illustrated in this flight deck view of an Air Gambia 707, is gradually giving way in modern jets to 'glass cockpits', which use television screens to project multi-function displays. A take-off and landing checklist is also shown beside the flight engineer's panel located behind the co-pilot's seat

Above A Saudi Arabian registered Boeing 707-321B sits forlornly at Manston, bereft of its tail and wings. Once named 'Clipper Yankee' and part of the prestigious Pan American fleet, the jet was bought by Saudi Arabian Prince Turki in 1987 and converted into a flying palace. Unfortunately a check revealed extensive corrosion and it was immediately positioned from Stansted to Manston, where it stands to this day. The interior is still fitted out with everything a Prince would want from plush fittings to gold-plated taps!

Right A ventral fin was fixed beneath the tail of many 707s after early flight test revealed directional stability problems. The fin also helped prevent pilots from over-rotating the aircraft on take-off. A number of Comet accidents at the time were attributed to over-rotation, and Boeing was anxious to avoid replicationg these disasters

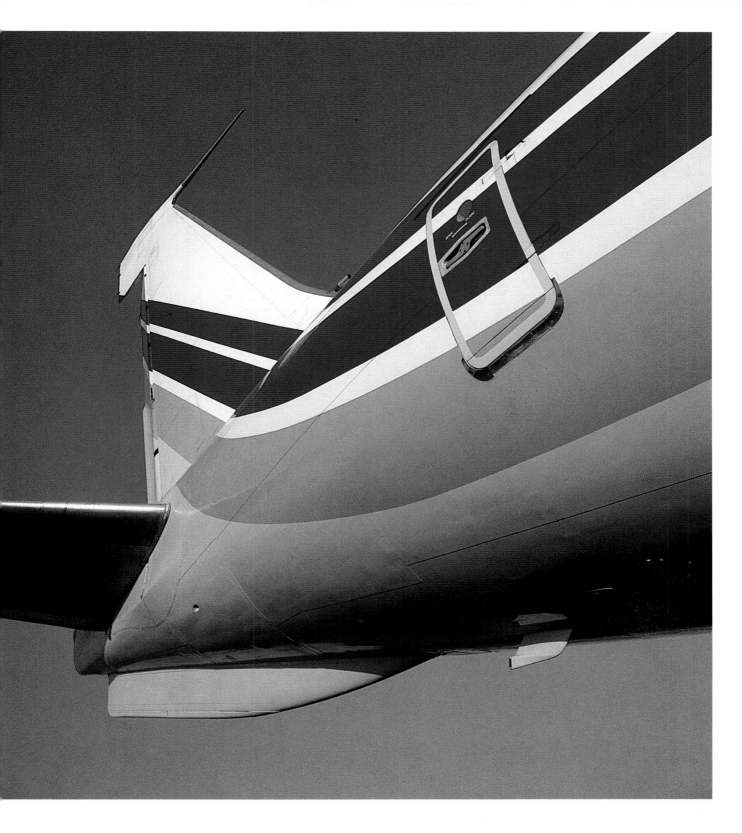

Douglas DC-8

These pages and overleaf Veteran DC-8-55F 9G-MKC trundles towards the take off point on Manston's extra wide runway, in readiness for an air-to-air photo shoot in August 1993. Douglas took a big gamble when it launched the DC-8 in 1955. It lacked the large jet bomber experience that Boeing had gained with the B-47 and B-52, and the prototype 707 was already flying when the decision to go ahead with the DC-8 was made. As a result, Douglas decided it did not have the time to develop a dedicated prototype and the first DC-8 to fly in 1958 was a production model. This -55F is a member of the DC-8F Jet Trader family which was designed as a set of combined freighter and passenger aircraft. The first version, the -54F, flew in October 1962 and a few still survive in service today. The -55F was designed for a maximum payload of more than 95,000 lbs (43,000 kg), and trans-Atlantic range in both directions. It was powered by Pratt & Whitney JT3D-3B engines, which were slightly improved versions of the 18,000 lb thrust variants on the -54. This particular aircraft is operated by London Gatwick-based MK Cargo Airlines on a handful of scheduled routes, plus ad-hoc services to virtually any destination depending on where it can find a cargo. Delivered initially to Seaboard World Airlines in 1964, it later saw service with the French *l'Armée de l'Air* and the Government of Togo. It is now mainly based out of Ostende, in Belgium, and Luxembourg

DOUGLAS DC-8 SERIES 50

(specification similar to Series 40, as run on page 50, except in the following particulars)

Weight: maximum 147,415 kg (325,000 lb); empty 60,020 kg (132,325 lb)

Powerplant: four 7718-kg (17,000-lb) Pratt & Whitney JT3D-1 two-shaft turbofans, later usually uprated to 8165-kg (18,000-lb) JT3D-3s

Performance: range with maximum payload and no reserves 11,260 km (7000 miles)

Production: 87, plus 3 converted from Series 30, plus 54 Jet Trader cargo versions

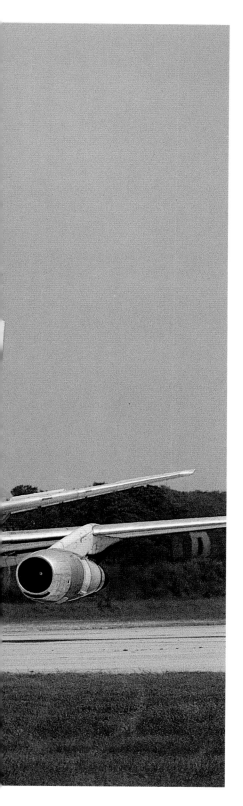

Above Exhaust plumes from four turbofans merge with the heat of the desert evening as Burlington Express DC-8-71 N8098U lines up for take-off from Phoenix Sky Harbour airport in April 1993. The overall performance of the stretched 'Super DC-8' models was revolutionised when a modification specialist, Cammacorp, replaced the aircraft's existing Pratt & Whitney JT3D engines with four CFM International CFM56-2-C5s. Take-off, climb and cruise altitude performance is vastly improved as a result of the new engines, and flights with higher gross weights than were possible with the original engines are routinely performed from hot and high elevation runways like this one in Arizona. This DC-8 was originally delivered to United Air Lines in 1969, and stayed in service with them until 1991 following conversion from -61 to -71 configuration in 1983

Left The long range and relatively large payload capability of the DC-8-61 made it an ideal charter aircraft for the North American market. This -61, photographed as it prepared for take-off from London Gatwick in the summer of 1989, was on lease from Airborne Express to Nationair, a privately owned Canadian carrier

Above and left The distinctive ram-air intakes under the nose of the DC-8 suggest a set of crooked teeth in these close-up views of a -63CF parked on the cargo ramp at Los Angeles International. The DC-8 is a workhorse of the air cargo industry and is cherished by most freight carriers for its excellent payload/range capabilities. Emery Worldwide Airlines, the operator of this aircraft, N959R, flies more than 30 DC-8s on domestic and international services. The bulk of its 'Super 63' fleet (15) have been converted into the re-engined -73 version, but 11 retain their original powerplants. The 'Super 63' was the largest member of the DC-8 family and flew for the first time in April 1967. At 187.4 ft in length and with capacity for 259 passengers it was the largest commercial airliner in service until the arrival of the Boeing 747 two years later. Having originally been designed for high-density, inter-continental passenger services, McDonnell Douglas recognised the great potential for the aircraft as a long distance cargo carrier. As a result, it designed a strengthened floor, cargo handling system and large 85 in by 140 in cargo door for the popular freighter conversion. Almost all the DC-8s still in service today are cargo versions, and they form the backbone of this ever-growing industry

Above A set of well-used main undercarriage tyres occupy the Miami ramp alongside a beautifully turned out DC-8-54F in March 1988. Andes Airlines was operating the freighter on lease from ARCA Columbia at the time, and in 1989 it passed into the hands of Venezuala-based cargo carrier Zuliana. The airline now operates the sole DC-8 on services from Maracaibo to Medellin and Bogota. This aircraft first flew in late 1962 and was delivered to Trans Canada Airlines as CF-TJL in April 1963. Air Canada, which absorbed TCA in 1964, continued to operate the aircraft for another 20 years. It subsequently passed through the hands of several operators, including Cargolux, before ending up in Central America. Due largely to its proximity to Central and South America, Miami is as much a haven for noisy stage 1 and 2 'geriatric jets' like the DC-8 and 707 as it is for piston-engined veterans like the DC-6 and DC-7, some of which occupy the ramp space in the background of this shot

Right Some DC-8s still 'soldier on' as military aircraft. The French *l'Armée de l'Air* operates several DC-8s on transport duties, and has converted some to perform the electronic reconnaissance role. This particular aircraft, F-RAFA/45820, is dwarfed by the elegant control tower at Paris Charles de Gaulle, where it was photographed shortly before its sale to Canada for commercial use by World Wide Charter Transport Systems as C-FIWW in September 1989. The aircraft, a -55F version, was originally delivered to French airline UTA in late December 1965, but was immediately bought for use by the French air force. A single DC-8 is equipped with a sophisticated set of signal intelligence (SIGINT) gear for 'snooping' on the enemy's electronic communications. An updated version of the system, called SARIGUE (systeme aeroporte de recueil d'information de guerre electronique) is expected to be placed aboard one of the force's DC-8-55CF transports sometime in the near future

DOUGLAS DC-8 SERIES 40

Type: medium-range passenger transport

Span: 43.41 m (142 ft 5 in)

Length: 45.87 m (150 ft 6 in)

Height: 12.91 m (42 ft 4 in)

Wing area: 257.6 m² (2773 sq ft)

Weight: maximum 142,880 kg (315,000 lb); empty 60,068 kg (132,425 lb)

Powerplant: four 7945-kg (17,500-lb) Rolls-Royce Conway 509 two-shaft turbofans, later uprated to 8165-kg (18,000-lb) Conway 509As

Performance: range with maximum payload and no reserves 9817 km (6100 miles)

Payload: 15,585 kg (34,360 lb); seats for up to 179 passengers

Crew: three to five

Production: 32

Above Still bearing tell-tale signs of its former European-based life, this battered looking DC-8-43 retains traces of its Alitalia livery a full 12 years after being purchased by ARCA Colombia. The airline also purchased ex-Braniff and Air Canada DC-8s, as well as three from Alitalia and cannabilised several to keep a few flying. This aircraft, believed to be the former Alitalia airliner I-DIWP, is seen at Miami in 1988. In the background stand the DC-8's progenitors, the DC-6 and DC-7. The ultimate version of the DC-7, the -7C did not enter service until 1956, two years after the first flight of the prototype Boeing 707. Douglas realised it was soon going to be left behind and decided to embark on a jet airliner of its own. Work started on the first DC-8 in February 1957 and it made its maiden flight from new production facilities at Long Beach, California, on 30 May 1958. The DC-8 line was shut down on 17 May 1972 after 556 jets had been produced

Right Their bright liveries still gleaming in the strong spring sunlight, these ex-Hawaiian Airlines DC-8-62Hs formed a fraction of the vast fleet of 'desert flowers' stored in the arid southwestern US at the beginning of 1993. A former United Air Lines aircraft, N8969U was one of three Hawaiian DC-8s stored at Kingman Field, Arizona, in April 1993. The 'Super 62' was designed for ultra-long range flights of up to 6500 miles, and had the same large wing and fuel reserves as the Intercontinental Super 63, but a fuselage 30 ft shorter. The 157.4 ft long aircraft could carry a maximum of 189 passengers compared with 259 in the longer version

DOUGLAS DC-8 SUPER 71F/73

(specification similar to Super 63CF/F, as run on page 57, except in the following particulars)

Powerplant: four 9979-kg (22,000-lb) CFM56 two-shaft turbofans

Performance: dramatically shorter take-off, steeper climb, reduced noise and lower fuel consumption than Super 63; range with maximum payload increased by 1400 km (870 miles); for range of 7600 km (4722 miles) payload with full reserves is increased from 20,400 kg (45,000 lb) to 25,850 kg (57,000 lb) or 280 passengers and baggage

Production: Over 100 conversions of Super 60 and -63 series aircraft carried out in the 1980s

Left Four CFM56s whine overhead as a United Parcel Service DC-8-71F coasts in to touchdown at New York's John F Kennedy international airport on an April evening in 1991. The multi-million dollar re-engining programme ensures not only better performance but also compliance with tough stage 3 noise laws. Those carriers that opted to buy or retain re-engined aircraft have a long term commitment to operate them well beyond 2000. This aircraft, N748UP, was first delivered to Saturn Airways in December 1967 and in its varied career has been operated by Seaboard World, Trans International, Capitol International, Flying Tiger Line and Emery Worldwide, before being converted to -71F configuration in 1985. All UPS -70 series aircraft are also being fitted with an upgraded 'glass' cockpit

Above A UPS DC-8-71 negotiates the notorious turn onto short finals at Hong Kong's Kai Tak airport in February 1992. The aircraft aim for a giant red and white chequerboard on a steep hillside not too far from the airport, before making the relatively tight turn at low-level over the crowded tenement blocks, shops and offices of Kowloon

Above Contrasting images of LAX are captured in this late night shot of the cargo ramp area. A brightly painted Connie Kalitta DC-8-51 stands against the backdrop of modern office blocks on Imperial Highway, and the curiously anachronistic Spanish Mission-style building known as 'Hangar One'. It is the only original building still standing at LAX dating from the days of the airport's dedication in 1929. On one side it had large articulated hangar doors which were opened to allow Ford Trimotors to be stored inside. In those times, LAX was known as Mines Field. Unfortunately there is no great mystery or myth behind this name – it is simply the surname of the real estate agent who sold the land to the City of Los Angeles

Right This DC-8-55 belongs to American global Airlines, formerly named Connie Kalitta Services after the wife of the carrier's original president and chief executive officer. American International operates international cargo charters with a fleet of Boeing 747s, 727s, DC-8s and DC-9s. Of 14 DC-8s in the fleet, 10 are -50 series. This well turned out aircraft, N807CK, was delivered to SAS as 'Harald Viking' in 1966 and served the Scandanavian carrier until 1980. It flew with various operators until 1988 when acquired by Connie Kalitta

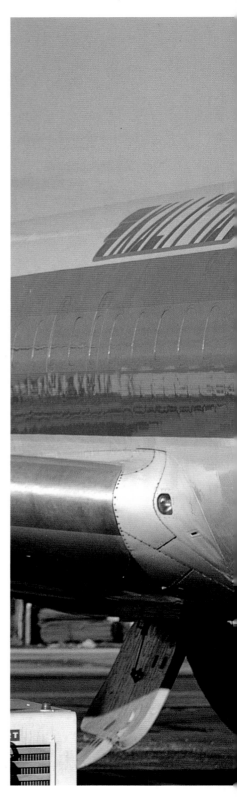

Above Crisp winter sunshine glints off the polished aluminium underside of Arrow Air DC-8-62F N802BN as it powers over the runway threshold of London Heathrow in January 1991. The silhouetted double slotted Douglas flaps are fully deployed, the portions that lie directly aft of the engines being hinged up to clear the jet blast. This aircraft, built as a -62H, spent from 1967 to 1978 with Alitalia before passing to Braniff Airways. It then served time with several operators including Hawaiian and Aeromexico, before being withdrawn from use and stored at Miami. Fortune smiled on the jet, however, and it was brought out of storage and converted to a -62F in March 1989. Arrow Air leased it in 1990

Right The sheer length of the Super 63 is accentuated in this view of an Arrow Air DC-8-63CF being towed across the Miami ramp in 1988. When McDonnell Douglas began looking at designs for what was to become the DC-10 it canvassed airlines with yet another stretch of the durable DC-8 airframe. The resulting design, internally dubbed the DC-8-83, added a further 19 ft to the -63 version. This produced a very thin aircraft some 206 ft in length, just around 20 ft shorter than a 747. Airlines had become used to the in-flight bending and flexing of the DC-8 Super 60 series but told McDonnell Douglas to go back to the drawing board when it suggested a further stretch!

DOUGLAS DC-8 SUPER 63

(specification similar to Super 62, as run on page 66, except in the following particulars)

Length: 57.12 m (187 ft 5 in)

Weight: maximum 158,750 kg (350,000 lb) (-63F and -CF 161,028 kg [355,000 lb]); empty 69,739 kg (153,749 lb)

Peformance: range with maximum payload and normal airline reserves 7240 km (4500 miles)

Payload: 30,719 kg (67,735 lb); seats for up to 259 passengers; (-63F and -CF 53,788 kg [118,583 lb] cargo)

Production: 41 plus 66 -F and -CF cargo and convertible versions

Above Throttles against the stops as a Pratt & Whitney JT3D-powered DC-8 climbs out over the Pacific Ocean to chase the setting sun. This shot, taken at Los Angeles in April 1993, may be a disturbing sight to the environmentally conscious Californians, but it is a lot better than it used to be. The exhaust of later DC-8s (and 707s) is nothing compared with the early years when the underpowered jets used thrust augmentation for take-off. Having ruled out the use of afterburners to boost thrust, Pratt & Whitney hit upon the use of water injection. This method involved injecting distilled water into the combustion chambers and reducing internal operating temperatures, thus allowing more fuel to be burned. The mass of water also fooled the engine into the illusion that more air was being sucked into the compressor. These modifications resulted in dramatically improved take-off thrust and shorter take-off runs. However, not only did it produce more noise, but it also created enough dense exhaust smoke to black out the entire length of the runway after each departure. The aircraft also had to be replenished with thousands of gallons of distilled water before every take-off, which reduced the amount of fuel, cargo and passengers that could be taken, and was thus a major inconvenience

Right A DC-8 approaches Miami out of a dramatic Florida sunset. Note how the vortices from the wingtips twist the trailing smoke produced by the engine exhaust

Left A DC-8 of Air Transport International opens its cavernous cargo door to swallow another load at Orlando, Florida. ATI provides worldwide cargo charter services for the express-package industry, as well as for the US Department of Defense and automotive manufacturers. Based in Little Rock, Arkansas, ATI operates a mixed fleet of eight DC-8-61F, -62F and -63Fs, and plans to operate three DC-8-71Fs and a -73F. It also expects to introduce a leased 747-100F into service shortly

Right The striped tail insignia of Airborne Express emblazoned across the tails of two DC-8s make them a distinctive sight as they stand side-by-side on the cargo ramp on the south side of Los Angeles International. Airborne Express operates 23 DC-8s and 46 DC-9s on a network of overnight small package services from its hub in Wilmington, Ohio. The network, which began operating in 1980, links more than 180 countries

Above A DC-8-54F on lease to CF Airfreight nears the end of its journey on a spring day in 1988. In a moment N141RD will touch down on Miami International's runway 9 Left

Above and left Delta was fond of its DC-8s and operated re-engined aircraft until the late 1980s. United Parcel Service now flies this aircraft as N744UP, having converted it to DC-8-71F configuration in November 1988. As N825E, this DC-8 served Delta for 20 years, the last five seeing the jet powered by CFM56 turbofans. The re-engining decision was a smart move for big operators like Delta. The DC-8 was a difficult aircraft to replace and, apart from the operational benefits of the new engines, it gave the carrier a breathing space until the arrival of new equipment like the MD-11. It also made the aircraft a lot easier to sell and, in most cases, more than doubled its re-sale value. This aircraft is pictured on final approach and flare at Miami in 1988 at the very end of its career as a passenger carrier

Above Mexicana DC-8-71F N8705J is captured by the camera accelerating through 170 kts as it climbs out of Los Angeles on an April day in 1993. At a fully loaded take-off weight of 147,400 kg, the -71F pilot can count on using up at least 2740 m of runway when taking off in still air and high temperatures from an airport at sea level like LAX. If the old engines were used under the same conditions the crew would need much more of the 12,000 ft runway. This particular DC-8 was on lease to Mexicana from Southern Air Transport, who in turn had leased it from the GPA Group. The aircraft first flew in 1969 and served United Air Lines for 21 years, seven of which were with CFM56 power. On its retirement from UAL in 1990 it was converted to -71F configuration

Above right Heading for sunshine, this Hawaiian Airlines DC-8-62H pushes back from the gate at Zurich airport under an overcast October sky in 1988. The long range of the 'Super 60' series made the 'big eight' an attractive niche player even in the boom years of the widebody. This Hawaiian-operated aircraft was originally delivered to United Air Lines in 1969 as N8970U 'Hilo Hattie'. It flew in UAL colours for 15 years before passing through the hands of Arrow Air to Hawaiian. It is now operating out of Australia as VH-BMR for Australian Consolidated Press

Right Rock stars, basketball teams and cast members from *Star Trek – The Next Generation* are frequent flyers on MGM Grand Air's fleet of up-market aircraft. The airline operates special charters, and what it calls 'super quality' passenger services, between LA and New York aimed at attracting 'show biz', film industry and sporting personalities. A wholly-owned subsidiary of entertainment conglomerate Metro-Goldwyn-Mayer, MGM Grand Air uses DC-8s fitted with only 35 first and 40 'coach' class seats to tailor to clientele who are used to leading 'lifestyles of the rich and famous'. Here, MGM Grand Air DC-8-62H N803MG receives attention from Page Avjet of Orlando in April 1990. The aircraft started out as Alitalia's 'Gioacchino Rossini' in 1967 and survived two periods of storage before eventually being bought

Above Rich International's natural aluminium finish on this DC-8-62 blends into the metallic glare of the Miami International concrete ramp on an overcast day early in 1988. This aircraft, N1805, was originally intended for Pan Am but the order was not taken up and it went instead to Braniff. Rich International leased it in 1983 and bought it two years later. Miami-based Rich International operate three DC-8-62/63s and three Lockheed L-1011 Tristars on charter services

Right The long fuselage of Aero Peru DC-8-62H 'Armando Revoredo' reflects the Florida evening light as it is replenished with stores for its return flight from Miami to Lima in March 1988. One of the last DC-8s built, OB-R1210 has flown for Aero Peru since 1981 when it was bought from Alitalia. The jet was delivered from Long Beach to Italy as I-DIWX 'Luigi Cherubini' in March 1971

DOUGLAS DC-8 SUPER 62

(specification similar to Super 61, as run on page 69, except in the following particulars)

Span: 45.23 m (148 ft 5 in)
Length: 47.98 m (157 ft 5 in)
Wing area: 271.9 m² (2927 sq ft)
Weight: maximum 151,950 kg (335,000 lb); empty 64,366 kg (141 903 lb)
Powerplant: four 8618-kg (19,000-lb) JT3D07s
Performance: range with maximum payload and normal airline reserves 9640 km (6000 miles)
Payload: 21,470 kg (47,335 lb); seats for up to 189 passengers
Production: 52 plus 16 F and CF cargo and convertible versions

Above The bright colours of Surinam Airways DC-8-62 caught by the camera on a busy sun-drenched day at Miami. Braniff Airways used the aircraft from 1969 to 1981, followed in 1983 by Arrow Air. Surinam Airways leased it the following year and named it 'Fajalobi' in 1986 following its outright acquisition. Later re-named 'Anthony Nesty', it was destroyed when it crashed on approach to its base at Paramaribo in June 1989

Above The personification of a 'stretch 8', this DC-8-61 sits in front of the engine test cells at Stansted Airport in September 1985. The aircraft belonged to National Airlines, formerly Overseas National Airways, at the time, and was on lease to now defunct Icelandic carrier Eagle Air (Arnarflug). The DC-8 was operated briefly by Spanish charter operator Spantax, before being bought by Airborne Express and re-registered N841AX

DOUGLAS DC-8 SUPER 61

(Specification similar to Series 40, as run on page 50, except in the following particulars)

Length: 57.12 m (187 ft 5 in)
Height: 12.92 m (42 ft 5 in)
Wing area: 267.9 m² (2884 sq ft)
Weight: maximum 147,415 kg (325,000 lb); empty 67,538 kg (148,897 lb)
Powerplant: four 8165-kg (18,000-lb) JT3D-3s
Performance: range with maximum payload and normal airline reserves 6035 km (3750 miles)
Payload: 30,240 kg (66,665 lb); seats for up to 259 passengers

Trijets

Left Pacific coast twilight bathes a United Air Lines Boeing 727-222 as it begins its take-off roll at Los Angeles International for an evening flight in May 1993. United's 33-year association with the Boeing trijet is second only to now-defunct Eastern Airlines, which placed the launch order for the type in November 1960. One of United's first 727s, a -22 delivered in 1964 and registered N7001U, returned to Seattle in 1991 where it was given to the Boeing-supported Museum of Flight Foundation. The aircraft is now stored at Everett where the museum's large aircraft annex is to be built

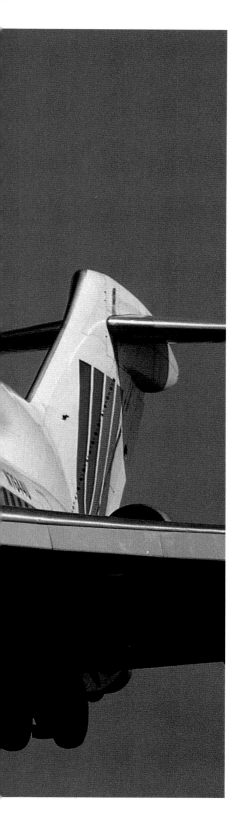

Left A United Air Lines Boeing 727-222 displays its impressive array of high-lift devices on final approach to London Heathrow during an early spring morning in 1993. The aircraft pictured, N7644U, was delivered to United in May 1969, and in recent years has become a common sight in European skies following the airline's take-over of Pan Am's UK – German services. The 727 was the first commercial airliner to be fitted with triple-slotted trailing edge flaps. These intricately engineered flap systems, added to the full-span leading-edge flap, increase wing area by 25 per cent when fully deployed, and help dramatically reduce the 727's take-off and landing distances. Boeing designed the 727 with such elaborate high-lift systems to meet Eastern Airline's exacting short field requirement. Eastern insisted that the 727 should be able to take off fully loaded and land safely on runway 4/22 at New York LaGuardia airport. At the time this was the only airfield in the US equipped with an instrument landing system. The runway itself was quite unique at a length of only 4860 ft

BOEING 727-200

Type: short/medium-range passenger and cargo transport
Span: 32.92 m (108 ft)
Length: 46.69 m (153 ft 2 in)
Height: 10.36 m (34 ft)
Wing area: 157.9 m² (1700 sq ft)
Weight: maximum originally 83,820 kg (184,800 lb), (Advanced 200) 86,405 kg (190,500 lb); empty originally 44,271 kg (97,600 lb), (Advanced) 44,815 kg (98,800 lb)
Powerplant: standard fitting, three 6577-kg (14,500-lb) st Pratt & Whitney JT8D-9A two-shaft turbofans; customer option of 7031-kg (15,500-lb) JT8D-15s, 7258-kg (16,000-lb) JT8D-17s or JT8D-17Rs with special emergency rating of 7893-kg (17,400-lb)
Performance: maximum cruising speed 953 km/h (592 mph); economical cruising speed 917 km/h (570 mph); range with payload of 18,144 kg (40,000 lb) and full reserves, originally 2685 km (1670 miles), (Advanced) 2970 km (1845 miles), current aircraft 3966 km (2464 miles)
Payload: structurally limited to 18,144 kg (40,000 lb); seats for up to 189 passengers
Crew: three
Production: 1260

Above 'Shades on. Let's go!' Sun-glasses protect the eyes of the United Air Lines Boeing 727-222 crew against the metallic glare of a spring day at LAX in 1993. A Northwest Airlines McDonnell Douglas DC-10-30 has taken up station on the taxyway behind the United 'three-holer'

Right Fading into the sunset? The onset of strict noise legislation will mean the end for many 727s by the year 2000, but ironically the same rules have triggered upgrade programmes which will prolong the lives of some aircraft by a further 20 years. The most comprehensive upgrade is produced by the Texas-based Dee Howard company, which replaces the 727-100's Pratt & Whitney JT8D-9 engines with Rolls-Royce Tay 650 turbofans. To date, United Parcel Service is the only customer of the programme, but others could follow as the 1999 noise deadline approaches. Boeing originally planned to power the 727 with the Rolls-Royce Spey, but was forced to abandon this when Eddie Rickenbacker, president of launch customer Eastern, refused to accept the idea. Boeing then approached Pratt & Whitney, who developed the JT8D from a military engine. The JT8D has since become the best selling commercial jet engine in history, with more than 14,000 produced. This 727 is captured seconds away from touchdown on London Heathrow's runway 27 Left during a calm summer evening in 1988

BOEING 727-100

Type: short/medium-range passenger and cargo transport
Span: 32.92 m (108 ft)
Length: 40.59 m (133 ft 2 in)
Height: 10.36 m (34 ft)
Wing area: 157.9 m² (1700 sq ft)
Weight: maximum (early production) 72,575 kg (160,000 lb); (later) 76,655 kg (169,000 lb); empty (early) 39,734 kg (87,600 lb); (-100C) 41,322 kg (91,100 lb)
Powerplant: three Pratt & Whitney JT8D two-shaft turbofans; originally 6350-kg (14,000-lb) st JT8D-1s, later option of 6577-kg (14,500-lb) JT8D-9s
Payload: varying from 13,154 kg (29,000 lb) for early deliveries to 15,649 kg (34,500 lb) at higher weight and to 19,958 kg (44,000 lb) for all-cargo 100C; seats for up to 131 passengers
Crew: three
Production: (-100) 407; (-100C and -QC) 164

Above left This scene captures the fatal turning point in the career of this Boeing 727-51. Having flown for almost a year on sub-lease for Suncoast Airlines, the aircraft was photographed at Fort Lauderdale – Hollywood Airport in March 1988, awaiting employment with Florida National Airlines. Unfortunately for this 727, the US-based work never came, and it was later flown to Istanbul, Turkey, where it was stored for several years before being broken up in 1992. This 727 first flew in March 1965 and was delivered the same month to Northwest Orient Airlines as N466US. In 1978 it was bought by Piedmont Airlines, and from 1983 until its demise, changed hands almost 20 times. The earlier short-fuselage version has not retained the high second-hand values associated with stretched late-build 727-200 and -200 Advanced airframes built towards the end of the production line in 1984

Above Pan American World Airways Boeing 727-235 'Clipper Quick Step' rotates from the runway at Miami International on a March afternoon in 1988. Almost 20 years old at the time this photograph was taken, N4749 had already seen 12 years of service with National Airlines when the carrier merged with Pan Am in 1980. As Pan Am's fortunes stumbled, 'Clipper Quick Step' was one of several aircraft to be sold to a financial corporation and leased back. When the airline failed altogether in 1991, the 727 became unemployed until January 1992 when it was leased to Braniff International Airlines

Above A ground power unit pumps energy into a stationary Boeing 727-22C as it sits on the ramp at Orlando, Florida. The 727 was actually the first jet airliner to be equipped with an auxiliary power unit and integral airstairs, thereby giving it independence from ground equipment such as that shown in this photograph. Used by Emery Worldwide Airlines for hauling cargo, this 727 was originally delivered as a passenger aircraft to United Air Lines in 1966. After a brief spell in South America with SAM Columbia (sub-leased via Avianca) during 1981, the trijet returned to the US later that same year and entered service with Emery. The side-loading cargo door can be distinguished mid-way along the forward fuselage

Left When prototype 727 E-1 ('E' for Eastern) made its maiden flight on 9 February 1963, one of the more unexpected phenomena experienced was a series of compressor stalls in the centre engine. The problem was traced to turbulent airflow caused by the oval shape of the intake in the tail-mounted number two engine. As can be seen from this photograph of an Evergreen International Airlines Boeing 727-30C, the company decided to stick with the original external design which remains a distinctive feature of the shorter - 100 series. The turbulent flow characteristics, and the engine surges, were cured by lining the inside of the large snake-like 'S-duct' tube which feeds air to the engine, with vortex generators (VGs). These are tiny projections more frequently seen on the upper surfaces of wings, and in this case, the skin of the vertical tail. Each projection juts out through the slower moving air dragging along the surface into the layer of slightly faster moving air just above it. The VG causes the faster airstream to swirl into the slower one, so re-energising the flow and helping it to stick more smoothly to the surface. Evergreen 727 N726EV is former Lufthansa airliner D-ABIO 'Hagen' and is seen at New York's John F Kennedy International Airport in April 1991

Above Evening sunlight glints off Boeing 727-82C, N709DH, at Miami International during the spring of 1990. This DHL Worldwide Courier aircraft, formerly CS-TBO 'Costa do Sol' of Transportes Aereos Portugueses, first flew in November 1968 and went on to serve with TAP for more than 10 years. Picked out well by the low light is the complex array of leading edge slats and triple-slotted trailing edge flaps. The reverse thrust buckets on the number one Pratt & Whitney JT8D engine are also in the deployed position, as is the airstair door

Right The flight engineer's position is well illustrated in this dramatic night shot of an American Airlines Boeing 727-223 nosed up to the gate at one of the airline's major hubs, Raleigh-Durham Airport in North Carolina. The fact that the 727 needs a flight engineer has been one of the main reasons for its eventual departure from frontline airline service. American Airlines, which once had a mammoth number of 727-100s and -200s, is currently in the process of drastically reducing its fleet from more than 150 in 1993 to around 60 by the year 2000. One of several reasons given by the airline for retiring its faithful workhorse is the high operating costs of a three-man crew versus the efficiency of a two-man operation. With the exception of its McDonnell Douglas DC-10s, every other type in its fleet will have a two-man cockpit

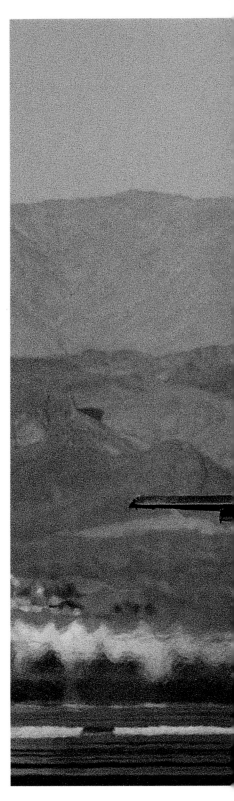

Above A classic image of a Boeing 727-200 in its original passenger configuration, photographed taxying at Miami International Airport in 1988. Aerovias Venezolanas, better known as Avensa, operates a large fleet of 727-100s and 727-200s from its Caracas headquarters. The Venezuelan carrier picked up this ex-Braniff Airways 727-227 in 1981, re-registering it YV-76C when it entered service. The aircraft was leased by fellow Venezuelan operator Servivensa in July 1991

Right A Boeing 727 launches into the evening sky over Las Vegas in April 1993 against the backdrop of the 5400-ft Muddy Mountains. The 727's steep 18° climb-out angle suprised many in the 1960s when it was first introduced into service, as most other types then flying passengers usually managed with a more sedate 15°

Right The UK's big trijet effort, the Hawker Siddeley (originally de Havilland 121) Trident, was commercially handicapped from the beginning because it was principally designed for the needs of just one airline, British European Airways (BEA). The story could have been so different. In 1959 BEA chairman, Lord Douglas, invited Boeing and Hawker Siddeley to combine the 727 and Trident programmes. Both companies sent engineering teams on exchange visits but a joint programme never materialised. Boeing believed the Trident was well designed but too restricted in size, range and power. BEA wanted the Trident to cruise at 600 mph (520 kts) over short-haul routes. Still wearing the colours of BEA's successor, British Airways, a retired Trident 3B stands forlornly as storm clouds gather to the west of London Heathrow in April 1986. The Trident 3B was the ultimate version of the trijet, 28 being produced between 1969 and 1975, when the last two were delivered to the Civil Aviation Administration of China. The engine exhaust visible is the Trident 3B's lesser known fourth engine. To boost climb out and take-off performance at maximum take-off weights of 150,000 lbs (52,395 kg), Hawker Siddeley built a small 5250-lb thrust Rolls-Royce RB.162-86 turbojet into the tail below the rudder. Like the -2E, the -3B was also fitted with three Rolls-Royce Spey RB.163-25 Mk 512s, each pumping out 11,950 lbs of thrust

HAWKER SIDDELEY TRIDENT 3

Type: short-range passenger transport
Span: 29.87 m (98 ft)
Length: 39.98 m (131 ft 2 in)
Height: 8.61 m (28 ft 3 in)
Wing area: 138.7 m² (1493 sq ft)
Weight: maximum 68,040 kg (150,000 lb); empty (152-seat) 37,090 kg (81,778 lb)
Powerplant: three 5425-kg (11,960-lb) st Rolls-Royce Spey 512-5W two-shaft turbofans, plus one 2381-kg (5250-lb) booster turbojet
Performance: typical high-speed cruise 936 km/h (581 mph); range with maximum payload and full reserves 1761 km (1094 miles)
Payload: 15,296 kg (33,722 lb); seats for up to 180 passengers
Crew: three
Production: 26

Above British Airways Trident 1C
G-ARPP pushing back at London
Heathrow in the early 1980s. 'Papa
Papa' first flew on 13 January 1965,
and served with BEA and later
British Airways before
ignominiously ending its days on the
Teesside airport fire dump in the UK
in 1983. On 10 June 1965 a BEA
Trident 1 made history by making
the first automatic touchdown on a
commercial airline service. The
Trident achieved this first using
Smiths Autoland equipment (now
part of GEC Marconi) at London
Heathrow

HAWKER SIDDELEY TRIDENT 1

Type: short-range passenger transport
Span: 27.38 m (89 ft 10 in)
Length: 34.97 m (114 ft 9 in)
Height: 8.23 m (27 ft)
Wing area: 126.16 m^2 (1358 sq ft)
Weight: maximum 52,163 kg (115,000 lb); empty 30,618 kg (67,500 lb)
Powerplant: three 4468-kg (9850-lb) st Rolls-Royce Spey 505 two-shaft
turbofans
Performance: typical high-speed cruise 948 km/h (589 mph); range with
maximum payload 1500 km (930 miles)
Payload: 9980 kg (22,000 lb); seats for up to 103 passengers
Crew: three
Production: 24

Above Full-flap and leading edge slats are deployed to slow British Airways Trident 2 G-AVFM as it nears the end of its journey to London Heathrow on a summer afternoon in July 1983. The aircraft was first delivered from the Hatfield production line in March 1969 and served with BEA and British Airways until 1984, when it was bought by Brunel Technical College. The same year it was withdrawn from airline use and began a new life as a ground training aid at Bristol Airport. The Trident 2 was a beefed-up version of the 1, with capacity for up to 115 passengers and more powerful Spey RB.163 engines. Although externally almost identical to the first versions, the 2 had a slightly increased wing span and low-drag wingtips. The last few operational Tridents still in service can be found flying with China United Airlines which operates nine. The vast majority of the 117 aircraft built have now been scrapped, but some are preserved in museums whilst the remains of others can be seen on airport firedumps across the UK

HAWKER SIDDELEY TRIDENT 2E

Type: short-range passenger transport
Span: 29.87 m (98 ft)
Length: 34.97 m (114 ft 9 in)
Height: 8.23 m (27 ft)
Wing area: 135.73 m² (1461 sq ft)
Weight: maximum 65,090 kg (143,500 lb); empty 33,203 kg (73,200 lb)
Powerplant: three 5411-kg (11,930-lb) st Rolls-Royce Spey 512-5W two-shaft turbofans
Performance: typical high-speed cruise 974 km/h (605 mph); range with maximum payload (space limited to 9697 kg [21,378 lb]) with full reserves 3910 kg (2430 miles)
Payload: 12,156 kg (26,800 lb); seats for up to 149 passengers
Crew: three
Production: 50

Twinjets

Right Boeing's baby jet, the 737, came close to being cancelled before it even flew, and yet it has become the best-selling jetliner in history with more than 3000 orders. Boeing was wary of proceeding with it because the Douglas DC-9 and BAC One Eleven had already been launched and between them had amassed around 300 orders. Lufthansa launched the 737 with an order for 22 737-100s in 1965 and United Air Lines lent its much-needed weight behind the programme in April of the same year by ordering 40 737-200s. Sales were slow, however, for several years and even up to the mid 1970s Boeing considered cancelling it. Orders for 1295 -100/200s were eventually taken before the line was closed in favour of the -300/400/500 versions. Photographed on approach to Miami in 1988, this United 737-222, christened 'City of Bakersfield', was originally delivered to the airline in 1968

Right Twenty four years after being delivered to United, N9068U looks as good as new in the airline's revamped livery as it manoeuvres for take-off at Los Angeles International in April 1993. Boeing was considering a T-tail design for the 737, which would have had aft-mounted engines like the DC-9. It rejected this in favour of the then novel under-wing design because the tail-mounted engines would have created more drag, thus slowing the 737. In addition, the new change reduced the structural weight and complexity of the wing as the weight of the engines provided bending relief by counteracting the upward force on the wing during flight. The initial wing design actually over-estimated this benefit and it had to be re-designed after failing in tests at 95 per cent of maximum load

BOEING 737

(data for Advanced 737-200)

Powerplant: two Pratt & Whitney JT8D-9A turbofan engines (each 14,500 lb; 6575 kg st); optionally, JT8D-15 engines (each 15,500 lb; 7030 kg st) or JT8D-17 engines (each 16,000 lb; 7257 kg st) or JT8D-17R engines (each 17,400 lb; 7892 kg st)

Wing span: 93 ft 0 ins (28.35 m)

Length overall: 100 ft 0 in (30.48 m); Cabin, including galley and toilet: length 68 ft 6 in (20.88 m); Max width 11 ft 7 in (3.53 m); Max height 7 ft 2 in (2.18 m); volume 4636 cu ft (131.28 m³)

Freight holds: forward 370 cu ft (10.48 m³), rear 505 cu ft (14.30 m³); max payload at brake release weight of 115,500 lb (52,390 kg): 34,400 lb (15,603 kg)

Max T-O weight: 117,000 lb (53,070 kg)

Max cruising speed: with JT8D-9A engines at an average cruise weight of 90,000 lbs (40,823 kg) at 22,600 ft (6890 m), 500 kts (576 mph; 927 km/h)

Rate of climb: at sea level, engines as above, at 100,000 lbs (45,355 kg) all up weight, 4200 ft (1280 m)/min

Range with max payload: at 30,000 ft (9145 m), including reserves for 174 nm (200 mile; 321 km) diversion and 45 min continued cruise, with 107 passengers, 2200 nm (2530 miles; 4075 km)

Accommodation: flight crew of two and seating for up to 130 passengers. Freight holds underfloor, forward and aft of wing

Variants:
Model 737-100: initial version (103 passengers) with JT8D-9 engines
Model 737-200: first 'stretched' version with lengthened fuselage
Model 737-200C: convertible passenger/cargo version
Model 737-200QC: quick-change version of 737-200C
Advanced 737-200: improved version introduced in 1969: aerodynamic and other refinements, permitting short-field operation

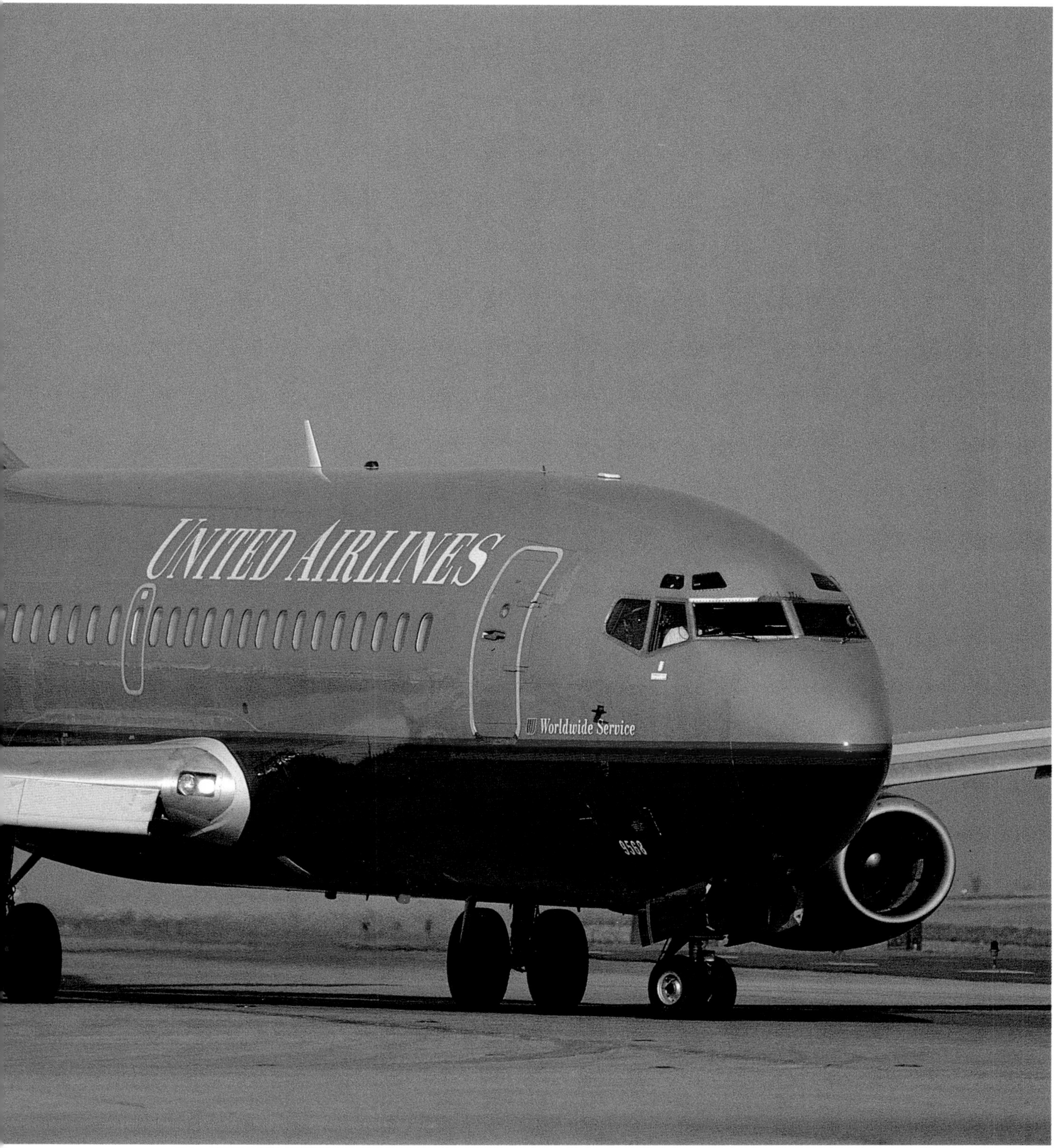
UNITED AIRLINES
Worldwide Service
9568

Above left The 737 has a good short-field performance thanks to high-lift devices on the wing and bucket-type thrust reversers. When it was first tested, however, the 737 was fitted with 727-style reversers which proved ineffective. The re-design cost $24 million but gave the 737 a dramatically improved short landing run. This helped promote sales to carriers like Pacific Western Airlines, who needed a rugged jet to operate from short strips in Canada. A former Pacific Western 737 is pictured landing at Fort Lauderdale, Florida, in 1988. At the time the aircraft was on lease to Presidential Airways and was carrying Republican senator Robert Dole during the 1988 Presidential campaign

Left An Inex Adria McDonnell Douglas DC-9-32 approaches London Gatwick after a flight from what was then Yugoslavia in October 1985. Since then both the airline and the country have changed names. Inex Adria reverted back to its original title, Aria Airways, in May 1986 when it became independent of the controlling Interexport group. The carrier had its licence to fly returned on 16 January 1992 following its removal the previous October by the Federal Secretariat of Transport and Communications at the height of the civil war in Yugoslavia. The new state of Slovenia emerged out of the war, and with international recognition of its new country, Adria resumed international services. This particular DC-9, YU-AHJ, was originally earmarked for service with Italian flag-carrier Alitalia, but was actually delivered to Inex Adria as 'Ljubijana' in April 1969. After 20 years service with the airline, including brief spells on lease with Egyptair and ZAS Airline of Egypt, the aircraft was re-registered SL-ABF on 26 December 1991 in recognition of its new nationality

Above Scandanavian Airline Systems DC-9-41 'Adils Viking' taxies to its gate at Paris Charles de Gaulle in June 1989. It was first delivered to SAS as SE-DBW in May 1968, and flew for the Scandanavian carrier until 1991. Northwest Airlines now operates this aircraft as N753NW. This version of the DC-9 is one of the prime candidates for major upgrades and re-engining that could extend its service life beyond 2010. The modification plan, called the DC-9X programme, involves beefing-up the keel structure and the area of skin around the engine pylon. If launched, the programme will also cover the installation of a modern cockpit based on that currently fitted in the MD-88

MCDONNELL DOUGLAS DC-9 SERIES 10 TO 40

(data for DC-9 Series 30)

Powerplant: two Pratt & Whitney JT8D-7 turbofan engines (each 14,000 lb; 6350 kg st); or JT8D-9 (14,500 lb; 6577 kg st); or JT8D-11 (15,000 lb; 6804 kg st); or JT8D-15 (15,500 lb; 7030 kg st); or JT8D-17 (16,000 lb; 7257 kg st)

Wing span: 93 ft 5 in (28.47 m)

Length overall: 119 ft 3 1/2 in (36.37 m)

Cabin: Length 71 ft 0 in (21.64 m) Max width 10 ft 1 in (3.07 m) Max height 6 ft 9 in (2.06 m)

Freight hold (underfloor): 895 cu ft (25.3 m³)

Max weight-limited payload: 28,094 lb (12,743 kg)

Max T-O weight: 121,000 lb (54,885 kg)

Max cruising speed: at 25 000 ft (7620 m) 490 kts (564 mph; 907 km/h)

Range: with 80 passengers and baggage at long-range cruising speed at 30,000 ft (9150 m), reserves for 100 nm (230 mile; 370 km) diversion and 45 min continued cruise at 30,000 ft, 1670 nm (1923 miles; 3095 km)

Accommodation: flight crew of two and seating for up to 119 passengers

Variants:

Series 10 Model 11: initial version (up to 90 passengers): 12,250 lb (5556 kg) st JT8D-5 turbofans

Series 20: 'hot and high' version, combining 90-passenger Series 10 fuselage with long-span wings of Srs 30 and JT8D-9 engines

Series 30: longer fuselage; increased-span wings with new high-lift devices; choice of JT8D-7/9/11/15/17 engines (see data). Built also for USAF (21) as C-9A Nightingale aeromedical transport; for USAF (3) as VC-9C special-mission transport; and for US Navy (14) and Kuwait Air Force (2) as C-9B Skytrain II fleet logistic support transport, combining features of Srs 30/40

Series 40: as Srs 30, but with longer fuselage (up to 132 passengers), increased fuel and JT9-D-9/15/17 engines

DC-9F/CF/RC: all-freight (F), convertible passenger/freight (CF) or mixed passenger/cargo (RC) versions of all current series

Left SAS DC-9-41 'Bent Viking' caught in the evening light as it nears touchdown at London Heathrow. Clearly shown is the 'double-bubble' fuselage shape used by Douglas engineers to maximise the internal capacity by mating two circular cross-sections of different widths. Also silhouetted against the evening sky is a foreign object damage (FOD) deflector located behind the nosewheel tyres. During the early years of DC-9 operation it was noted that the nosewheels would sometimes kick up gravel, stones and other debris from the runway during the take-off and landing roll. This debris could cause foreign object damage to the underside of the aircraft and even the engine, so Douglas engineers devised this simple mud-guard-like device to fit around the back of the wheels. Some variants also have guards around the main undercarriage wheels specifically to protect the engines, flaps and rear fuselage from damage

Right Nose mounted air data probes festoon KLM McDonnell Douglas DC-9-33RC 'City of Madrid' as it manoeuvres at London Heathrow in April 1986. KLM, (Koninklyke Luchtvaart Maatschappy) has been a loyal Douglas customer, operating virtually every commercial type that the company has produced from the DC-2 to the MD-11. It even made use of the almost unknown DC-5, buying a third of the total production run of 12. 'City of Madrid', registered PH-DNM, was delivered from Long Beach, California, to Schiphol airport, Amsterdam, in April 1968. The aircraft served in Europe for 19 years, before returning to the USA to begin a new career as a freighter

Above left Nicknamed the 'Sport' by some pilots because of its high thrust-to-weight ratio and sprightly performance, the smallest member of the Douglas twinjet family is represented here by a Finnair DC-9-15MC. This aircraft, the 165th DC-9 off the Long Beach line, was delivered to Texas International Airlines in September 1967 and bought by Finnair in 1972. Re-registered as OH-LYH, the aircraft operated cargo services for the Helsinki-based carrier until 1988, when it was bought by Evergreen International Airlines. It was later leased in 1990 to Air Sur as EC-489. Clearly visible as the -15 approaches London Heathrow in August 1987 is the cargo door cut into the forward fuselage

Left As the DC-9 family grew in size, Douglas introduced more high-lift devices to the wing to help the larger, heavier versions of the aircraft operate from the same small runways as the first variants. This shot of an Eastern DC-9-31 landing at Miami in March 1988 perfectly illustrates the extended full-span leading-edge slat fitted to the wing. This device was introduced on all models

from the -30 series onwards. N8920E, one of the first batch of -30s produced, served Eastern Air Lines for 21 years before being consigned to storage in the Arizona desert. It enjoyed a short reprieve on lease to Midway Airlines, but returned to storage when the Chicago-based carrier folded in November 1991

Above More Midway victims languish in the Arizona desert at the Kingman storage facility in April 1993. Flight deck windows, doors, hatches, engine and air conditioning intakes and other orifices are hermetically sealed to prevent dust and moisture penetrating the aircraft's systems and interior, thus preserving the aircraft in as good a condition as possible. This aircraft, DC-9-15 N45779, was returned to Polaris Aircraft Leasing Corporation by Midway just four months before the carrier folded. Polaris immediately placed it in storage, where it has remained ever since. The aircraft was originally delivered to Trans World Airlines as N1065T in March 1967

Above The Douglas twinjet gained a large stronghold in Europe as a popular short-to-medium range aircraft with major flag carriers such as SAS, KLM and Alitalia. Here Alitalia DC-9-32 I-DIBT taxies to the stand after arriving at Zurich airport on an autumn evening in 1988. Alitalia, the national airline of Italy, had flown the aircraft from new for 21 years when this atmospheric image was captured

Right With full flap deployed, this British Midland Airways (BMA) DC-9-15 was photographed on short finals seconds from touchdown at London Heathrow on a bright January day in 1991. BMA uses the aircraft on many of its shuttle services, and named this particular example (G-BMAB) 'The Mogul Diamond' after the famous gem when it launched its 'Diamond Class' service initiative. The aircraft was originally delivered to Trans World Airlines as N1057T in October 1966, and was bought by BMA in 1979 as a replacement for its Vickers Viscount fleet. The DC-9s, in turn, will be replaced by Fokker 70s and Fokker 100s

Left A head-on view of a DC-9-15 following the green centreline lights at Los Angeles International on an April evening in 1993. This is one of nine DC-9-14/15s operated by Mexico-based Aero California. Although predominantly a Mexican regional operator, the brightly coloured DC-9s are often seen fulfilling regular daily services to southwestern US airports like Phoenix Sky Harbour and LAX

Above BAC One-Eleven's continue to occupy a substantial niche in the US corporate fleet. Hilton Hotels Corporation bought One-Eleven 414EG from German

operator Bavaria Fluggesellschaft in 1975. The British-made twinjet first flew from the production line at Hurn in January 1970 and was delivered the following month to Germany as D-AILY 'Dominikus Zimmermann'. It was photographed at Las Vegas McCarran International airport in April 1993 against a background of stored DC-10s. Now coded N123H, it wears the markings of the official 'chase plane' of the Earthwinds around-the-world balloon attempt, which was partially sponsored by the hotel group. The One-Eleven's Rolls-Royce Spey engines are fitted with distinctive hushkits, which appear to elongate the nacelles

BAC ONE-ELEVEN SERIES 200, 300, 400 AND 475

Powerplant: two Rolls-Royce Spey Mk 512 DW turbofan engines (each 12,550 lb; 5692 kg st)

Wing span: 93 ft 6 in (28.50 m)

Length overall: 93 ft 6 in (28.50 m)

Cabin, excluding flight deck: length 56 ft 10 in (17.31 m); max width 10 ft 4 in (3.16 m); max height 6 ft 6 in (1.98 m)

Freight holds: forward 354 cu ft (10.02 m³) rear 156 cu ft (4.42 m³)

Max payload: 21,269 lb (9647 kg)

Max T-O weight: 92,000 to 98,500 lb (41,730 to 44,678 kg)

Max cruising speed: at 21,000 ft (6400 m) 470 kts (541 mph; 871 km/h)

Rate of climb: at sea level at 300 kts (345 mph; 555 km/h), 2480 ft (756 m)/min

Range: 1619 nm (1865 miles; 3000 km)

Accommodation: flight crew of two and seating for up to 89 passengers in single or mixed-class layouts. Two baggage and freight holds underfloor, fore and aft of wings

Variants:

Series 200: initial production model, with 10,330 lb (4686 kg) st Spey 25 Mk 506 turbofans and up to 89 passenger seats. Total of 56 built; entered service April 1965

Series 300: longer-range development of Srs 200, with 11,400 lb (5171 kg) st Spey Mk 511 engines (in longer nacelles) and increased standard fuel tankage. Nine built

Series 400: version of Srs 300 modified to US requirements, with lift dumpers and dropout emergency oxygen masks. Total of 69 built

Series 475: Combines standard fuselage and accommodation of Srs 400 with wings and powerplant of Srs 500 and modified landing gear. Large forward freight door available optionally

Left The Irish shamrock and green livery of Aer Lingus One-Eleven 208AL EI-ANG blends in against the background of rolling scenery around Bristol Airport as it flares for landing above runway 09 at the completion of flight EI 282 from Dublin. Once a common sight around European airports, this aircraft, christened 'St Declan', has since been sold by the Irish carrier, but four sister aircraft remain in service

Right The perfectly circular cross-section of the BAC One-Eleven fuselage is clearly evident in this night view of a Dan-Air aircraft at Bristol in 1985. Dan-Air, now absorbed by British Airways, bought the aircraft a decade earlier as G-BDAS from British Aircraft Corporation. The One-Eleven, 518FG, first flew in January 1970 and was delivered as 'Halcyon Sun' to Court Line Aviation. This holiday charter airline collapsed in 1974, and the twinjet was duly repossessed by BAC

Left Dan-Air London One-Eleven 301AG G-ATPK approaches London Gatwick in the spring of 1985. This aircraft dates from 1966 and has seen service with long gone carriers such as British Eagle International Airlines and Laker Airways, as well as spending time as a corporate jet with Hughes International, amongst others. The One-Eleven was sold to Nigerian operator Okada Air as 5N-OMO in 1991. The jet's large fowler flaps are fully deployed for landing in this photograph. With full-flap and at standing maximum landing weight, the aircraft's stall speed was just under 100 kts, or about 113 mph

Right Distinctive Spey hushkits and the angled exhaust of the auxiliary power unit help make the One-Eleven stand out from other twinjets. This view also accentuates the extra length of the -500 series, the largest version of the One-Eleven built. This British Airways-owned example first flew in 1968 and was delivered to British European Airways in April 1969. The -500 series were also the most powerful versions of the One-Eleven, and were equipped with Rolls-Royce Spey Mk 512-14 turbofans, each rated at around 12,500 lbs of thrust. Despite the available power, the APU was always left on to supply the cabin with air conditioning for take-off. This eliminated the performance penalty of bleeding off engine air for cabin air conditioning when as much engine power as possible was needed for take-off

BAC ONE-ELEVEN SERIES 500

Powerplant: two Rolls-Royce Spey Mk 512 DW turbofan engines (each 12,550 lb; 5692 kg st)

Wing span: 93 ft 6 in (28.50 m)

Length overall: 107 ft 0 in (32.61 m)

Cabin, excluding flight deck: length 70 ft 4 in (21.44 m); max width 10 ft 4 in (3.16 m); max height 6 ft 6 in (1.98 m)

Freight holds, total volume: 687 cu ft (19.45 m³)

Max payload: 26,418 lb (11,983 kg)

Max T-O weight: 99,650 to 104,500 lb (45,200 to 47,400 kg)

Max cruising speed: at 21,000 ft (6400 m), 470 kts (541 mph; 871 km/h)

Rate of climb: at sea level at 300 kts (345 mph; 555 km/h), 2280 ft (695 m)/min

Range: 1480 nm (1705 miles; 2744 km)

Accommodation: flight crew of two and seating for up to 119 passengers. Two baggage and freight holds underfloor, fore and aft of wings

Variant:

Series 500: 'stretched' version, derived from Srs 300/400; lengthened fuselage, extended wingtips, strengthened landing gear

Above The inherent sturdiness of the One-Eleven design convinced some that it would be viable to extend the type's life through re-engining. Texas-based Dee Howard modified this One-Eleven, a 401AK, with Rolls-Royce Tay turbofans in 1990. Dee Howard has since turned its attention to re-engining Boeing 727-100s with a variant of the same engine. Romanian manufacturer Romaero is also looking for investment to build -500s with Tay engines. These would be known as the Series 2560. The airframe used by Dee Howard for the programme was originally delivered to American Airlines in 1966 as N5019. American Airlines had been courted by both BAC and Douglas, the latter manufacturer offering their new DC-9, but they chose the One-Eleven when BAC promised a faster delivery schedule. The airline bought 30 One-Elevens in 1965 and 1966, but had disposed of them all by the end of 1972. It subsequently ordered 260 McDonnell Douglas MD-82/83 twinjets, which are the direct

ancestors of the DC-9! N5019 was used by many corporations as a business jet before being converted to One-Eleven 2400 standard. The modified aircraft, seen here at the Farnborough airshow in September 1990, is ballasted at the nose to offset the weight of the heavier Tay engines in the tail

Above right The distinctive Sud-Aviation SE.210 Caravelle pioneered the design of transports with tail-mounted jet engines. Here, an Istanbul Airlines Caravelle 10R is caught between flights on a sticky day at Istanbul airport in August 1987. The aircraft, TC-AKA, was originally delivered to German operator Lufttransport-Unternehmen in July 1968, after which it spent the next 18 years flying for various German outfits before being leased to Istanbul Airlines in 1986. 'Kilo Alpha' ended its flying days in November 1991 when it was withdrawn from service and stored for spares at Ercan, Cyprus. The -

10R was the first version of the Caravelle not to be powered by the Rolls-Royce Avon turbojet, being fitted instead with with the more powerful 14,000-lb thrust Pratt & Whitney JT8D-1 engine developed originally for the Boeing 727

CARAVELLE 10R, 11 AND SUPER

(specification similar to Mk III, as run on page 110, except in the following particulars)

Length: (11) 32.71 m (107 ft 4 in); (Super) 33.01 m (108 ft 4 in)
Weight: maximum (10R) 52,000 kg (114,640 lb); (11) 54,000 kg (119,050 lb); (Super) 56,000 kg (123,460 lb); empty (10R) 29,075 kg (64,100 lb) (11) 28,841 kg (63,585 lb); (Super) 30,055 kg (66,260 lb)
Powerplant: two 6350-kg (14,000-lb) Pratt & Whitney JT8D-7 two-shaft turbofans
Performance: maximum cruising speed (10, 11) 800 km/h (497 mph); (Super) 835 km/h (518 mph); range with maximum payload and reserves (10R) 3455 km (2145 miles); (11) 2800 km (1740 miles); (Super) 2655 km (1650 miles)
Payload: (10R) 9400 kg (20,720 lb); (11) 9095 kb (20,050 lb); (Super) 9100 kg (20,060 lb); seats for 80 (10R), 99 (11) or 105 (Super)
Production: (10R) 20; (11) 6; (Super) 22

Above left Swiss-owned Caravelle 10R HB-ICO noses up to the gate at Zurich airport in October 1988. This view of the aircraft clearly illustrates how the Caravelle used the same cockpit and nose section design as the de Havilland Comet. Also highlighted by the sun angle are the large wing fences which are used to improve the air flow across the Caravelle's slightly swept wing. Operated at the time by Compagnie de Transport Aerien (CTA), this -10R first flew in December 1969 and was still in service in the early 1990s with Air Service Nantes

Left Flying into the sunset of its career, Caravelle F-GHKM had only seven months of service left when captured by the camera on finals to runway 27 at Bristol on an April evening in 1991. The aircraft first flew in 1969 and served for most of its career with Danish carrier Sterling as OY-STH, apart from a short spell on lease to Air Toulouse International when this shot was taken. It was withdrawn from service and stored at Copenhagen in late 1991

Above The French-built Caravelle VI-R attracted orders from United Air Lines, which took delivery of a fleet in 1961/62. N1001U was the first to enter service with

United in June 1961 as 'Ville de Toulouse', and ended up flying for the Western Geophysical Corporation. In UAL service the Caravelle was fitted out for 16 first class and 54 economy seats. It is pictured at Goodyear Litchfield, near Phoenix, Arizona, in March 1989. The following year it was donated to the Pima County Air Museum, located adjacent to the massive military storage area at Davis-Monthan Air Force Base in Tucson, Arizona. Caravelle VI-Rs were fitted with three-section spoilers near the trailing edge of the wing to kill lift on the landing roll-out and increase pressure on the wheels

CARAVELLE VI

(specification similar to Mk III except in the following particulars)

Weight: maximum (VIN) 48,000 kg (105,822 lb); (VIR) 50,000 kg (110,230 lb); empty (VIN) 27,330 kg (60,250 lb); (VIR) 28,655 kg (63,175 lb)

Powerplant: (VIN) two 5535-kg (12,200-lb) Avon 531s; (VIR) two 5725-kg (12,600-lb) Avon 533Rs

Performance: maximum cruising speed 845 km/h (525 mph); range 2350 km (1460 miles)

Payload: 8300 kg (18,080 lbs)

Production: 109

Above This fine looking Caravelle III now rots in Kinsahasa, Zaire, but is pictured in happier times at Paris Le Bourget in May 1985. Originally delivered to Royal Air Maroc as CN-CCT 'Tafraout' in August 1968, the Caravelle passed through several owners before being bought by Liberian-registered Atlantic Aviation Service Corporation, who's colours it appears in here

SUD-AVIATION SE.210 CARAVELLE III

Type: short-range passenger transport
Span: 34.3 m (112 ft 6 in)
Length: 32.01 m (105 ft)
Height: 8.72 m (28 ft 7 in)
Wing area: 146.7 m² (1579 sq ft)
Weight: maximum 46,000 kg (101,413 lb); empty 24,185 kg (53,320 lbs)
Powerplant: original Mk I, two 4763-kg (10,500-lb) st Rolls-Royce Avon 522 single-shaft turbojets; Mk III two 5170-kg (11,400-lb) Avon 527s
Performance: maximum cruising speed 805 km/h (500 mph); range with maximum payload and reserves 1700 km (1056 miles)
Payload: 8400 kg (18,520 lbs); seats for up to 80 passengers
Crew: two to three
Production: 78, preceded by 20 Mk Is and 12 Mk IAs

Above Tupolev's ubiquitous Tu-134 still operates in large numbers throughout the former Soviet Union and its satellite states. Like many other communist members of the Soviet's bloc, Bulgaria's Balkan airline purchased its share of Tu-134s. This aircraft, a Tu-134A-3, is pictured at Moscow's Sheremtyevo airport during the summer of 1991. LZ-TUZ is powered by twin 15,000-lb thrust Aviadvigatel (formerly MKB) D-30-IIIs, fitted with clamshell thrust reversers to shorten the landing run

Left A classic cockpit view of the Tu-134A showing the tunnel through which the navigator crawls to the glazed nose section. This extraordinary feature is common to several early Soviet airliners of the same vintage, and indicates both the transport's former pseudo-military role and the widespread shortage of even primitive navigation aids. Also noticeable in this picture is the cumbersome looking autopilot system located in front of the centre window panel and above the tunnel entrance. The large device situated beside the pilot's seat is a weather radar display, complete with cathode ray tube. This is the cockpit of former Interflug Tu-134A DDR-SCK, which now resides in Augsburg's aircraft museum in Germany

Above right An all too common sight at any Russian airport. An Aeroflot Tu-134 stands idle at Moscow's Sheremetyevo airport with an engine casing open ready for maintenance. Many of the major Russian airfields are littered with carcasses of older Tu-134s which are often stripped of pieces to keep others flying. The aircraft's 3° downward wing droop, well illustrated in this August 1991 shot, is a distinctive feature of all large aircraft produced by the Tupolev Design Bureau over the Cold War years. This aircraft is powered by two Aviadvigatel D-30 II engines, which produce the same thrust levels as the IIIs used in the later Tu-134A-3, but at higher operating temperatures. Maintenance requirements are therefore greater for this type of engine, as evidenced in this shot

TUPOLEV Tu-134

(data for Tu-134A)

Powerplant: two Aviadvigatel D-30 turbofan engines (each 14,990 lb; 6800 kg st)

Wing span: 95 ft 2 in (29.01 m)

Length overall: 121 ft 6½ in (37.05 m)

Cabin: (Tu-134, portion containing seats only) length 45 ft 5½ in (13.85 m), width 8 ft 10½ in (2.71 m), height 6 ft 5 in (1.96 m), volume 1073 cu ft (58.70 m³)

Cabin volume (Tu-134A): 2400 cu ft (68.0 m³)

Max usable volume: (less flight deck) 3040 cu ft (86.10 m³)

Baggage compartment volume: forward 141-212 cu ft (4.0-6.0 m³) aft 300 cu ft (8.50 m³)

Max payload: 18,075 lbs (8200 kg)

Max T-O weight: 103,600 lbs (47,000 kg)

Max cruising speed: at 32,800 ft (10,000 m), all up weight of 92,600 lbs (42,000 kg): 477 kts (550 mph; 885 km/h)

Max rate of climb: at sea level, all up weight of 97,999 lbs (44,000 kg): 2913 ft (888 m)/min

Service ceiling: at max take-off weight: 39,000 ft (11,900 m)

Range: at max take-off weight with 8800-lb (4000 kg) payload, at 405 kts (466 mph; 750 km/h) at 32,800 ft (10,000 m), with 1 hr fuel reserves, 1890 nm (2175 miles; 3500 km)

Accommodation: flight crew of three and seating for up to 96 economy class passengers. Baggage compartment aft of the flight deck and a large baggage and freight compartment aft, in line with the engines

Variants:

Tu-134: initial version, with 114 ft 8 in (34.95 m) overall length and seats for up to 72 passengers

Tu-134A: 'stretched' version (see data) for up to 96 passenges in lengthened fuselage; thrust reversers, strengthened landing gear and other refinements

Above Aeroflot airliners were ready to operate under wartime conditions at very short notice. Here, a Tu-134A sports an identification, friend or foe (IFF) transceiver antenna on the anti-glare shield above the glazed nose. The SRO-2/2M IFF, or 'Odd Rods' as it is code-named by NATO, is more often seen on fully fledged combat types like the Mikoyan MiG-29 and Sukhoi Su-27. In the background, a three-engined Tu-154 appears in the evening twilight at what was then called Leningrad in 1991

Right Passengers board Aeroflot Tu-134A CCCP-65861 at Pulkovo airport, Leningrad, on a summer's day in 1991. Since then the aircraft has been re-registered and absorbed into Belavia, the new Belorussian carrier, and the city has reverted to its old name of St Petersburg

Above The first Soviet jet airliner was the Tupolev Tu-104. Like its contemporary, the British-made de Havilland Comet, the Tu-104 was designed with engines buried in the wing root to minimise drag. Early variants were powered by the primitive Mikulin AM-3A turbojet. Derived from the Tu-16 *Badger* bomber, the Tu-104 suffered acute problems with engine reliability and pressurisation system failures. A preserved example is mounted on a plinth opposite the terminal of Moscow's Vnukovo airport and is seen rising above the gathering rubbish on a summer's day in 1991

Right A very old looking Tupolev Tu-104A stands alongside an Ilyushin Il-18 as part of the impressive Monino museum collection outside Moscow in June 1991. To convert the Tu-16 bomber to a Tu-104 passenger aircraft, Tupolev had to add a new, taller fuselage to the same basic wing and engine configuration. Despite the re-design, the two main spars of the down-sloping wings passed through the cabin. This forced the designers to build a 'step' into the cabin floor, which is indicated from the outside on this aircraft by the higher location of two windows over the wing. Aeroflot also used a partially civilianised version of the Tu-16 *Badger*, called the Tu-104G, for high-speed mail carrying duties. The joint predecessor for both the Tu-104 and the Tu-16 was the Tu-88 prototype, which first flew in April 1952

TUPOLEV Tu-104

(data for Tu-104B)

Powerplant: two Mikulin AM-3M-500 turbojet engines (each 21,385 lbs; 9700 kg st)

Wing span: 113 ft 4 in (34.54 m)

Length overall: 131 ft 5 in (40.06 m)

Cabin: excluding flight deck, galley, toilets etc, length 66 ft 0 in (20.12 m), max width 10 ft 6 in (3.20 m), max height 6 ft 5 in (1.95 m)

Max payload: 26,455 lbs (12,000 kg)

Max T-O weight: 167,550 lbs (76,000 kg)

Max cruising speed: 486 kts (560 mph; 900 km/h)

Service ceiling: 37,750 ft (11,500 m)

Range: 1130 nm (1305 miles; 2100 km)

Accommodation: Flight crew of five and seating for up to 100 passengers. Two large underfloor holds for up to 8820 lbs (4000 kg) of baggage and freight

Variants:

Tu-104: initial version for 50 passengers; overall length 127 ft 5½ in (38.85 m), 14,881-lb (6750 kg) st AM-3 engines. Adapted from Tu-16 bomber

Tu-104A: as Tu-104, but redesigned cabin seating up to 70 passengers, and AM-3M-500 engines

Tu-104B: 'stretched' version of Tu-104A (see data), seating up to 100 in longer fuselage

Rarities

Left Evening shadows creep over sand, scrub and a Convair CV-880 – fellow inhabitants of the huge jet storage site in California's Mojave desert. Convair believed it had a winner in the CV-880, and its successor the CV-990, because both were designed as 'hot ships', meant to outpace both the 707 and DC-8. Convair – now part of General Dynamics – announced plans in 1956 to develop a medium range jet airliner and flew the first aircraft from its San Diego production line in January 1959. As the aircraft used a big wing designed for a fast climb, Convair engineers decided there was no sense in wasting the space so they filled it with fuel tanks. As a result, Convair expected the CV-880 to perform economically from 300 to 3000 miles. The reality was somewhat different, however, and the CV-880, although reportedly excellent to fly, turned out to be a mechanical nightmare and expensive to maintain

Left A lone Convair CV-990 sits amongst the world's largest repository of surviving Convair 880s. The CV-990 although 10 ft longer than its predecessor, is more easily distinguished by the large anti-shock bodies extending back from the trailing edge of the wing. As part of Convair's quest for the highest speeds, it fitted the CV-990 with powerful General Electric CJ-805-21 aft fan engines. A derivative of the J79 selected specially for the CV-880 (known commercially as the CJ-805-3), the -21 was used on the Convair B-58 Hustler, which was then the world's fastest supersonic bomber. The CV-990 also had a thinner wing than the CV-880 and, combined with the more powerful engines, offered a potential top speed of Mach 0.91 and a design 'never exceed' speed of 0.92. However, in wind tunnel tests designers discovered that a shock wave developed over the trailing edge of the wing, producing drag. To cure the problem Convair developed the anti-shock bodies, or 'speed pods', and used the space to house more than 600 gallons of extra fuel in each wing. Just when Convair was feeling confident about meeting performance guarantees to American Airlines and Swissair, more problems cropped up on early test flights in 1961. A wing flutter – or bad vibration – problem occurred when the aircraft was at high speed and the outer pods were filled with fuel. It meant commercial disaster as the only cure was an engine re-alignment and this badly affected deliveries. Boeing and Douglas cleaned up and Convair only received 37 orders for the CV-990. Several of the 880s in this aerial view of Mojave in April 1993 still show traces of TWA livery. Howard Hughes, then the boss of the airline, was attracted by the high speed promises of the CV-880 and ordered 30

CONVAIR CV-880

Type: short/medium-range passenger transport
Span: 36.58 m (120 ft)
Length: 39.42 m (129 ft 4 in)
Height: 11.07 m (36 ft 4 in)
Wing area: 184.4 m² (1985 sq ft)
Weight: maximum 83,689 kg (184,500 lbs); empty 38,238 kg (84,300 lbs)
Powerplant: four 5080-kg (11,200-lb) st General Electric CJ-805-3 single-shaft turbojets (-880M, 5284-kg [11,650-lb] CJ-805-3Bs)
Performance: economical cruising speed 895 km/h (556 mph); range with maximum payload (-880M) 5150 km (3200 miles)
Payload: 9752 kg (21,500 lbs); seats for up to 110 passengers
Crew: three to four
Production: 65

Above A sad, scorched, Convair CV-880 sits in the sunshine at San Juan, Puerto Rico, where it serves as a training aid to the local firefighters. Formerly JA8026, this 880-22M-3 was delivered to Japan Air Lines as 'Yanagi' in July 1963. It served with various operators until leased by Profit Airlines as 'La Isla del Encanto' in August 1981. It was withdrawn from use and stored at San Juan in 1985, but still retains tell-tale signs of its last airline identity in this photograph, taken in March 1988. The CV-880 rudder, evident in this view, was balanced with weights made of sintered tungsten. The CV-990 rudder, which was powered, actually used uranium as a counterbalance because it is 165 per cent denser than other heavy materials like lead. Company manuals provided for operators at the time said the CV-990 rudder balance weights, 'are marked CAUTION – RADIOACTIVE MATERIAL – but they may be handled with complete safety'

Above The end was nigh for this Convair CV-990 when captured by the camera at Fort Lauderdale, Florida, in March 1988. Unfortunately, ownership by 'Christ is the Answer Inc' was not enough to save N990E from the cutter's torch, and it was broken up in Florida just over two years later. The aircraft had been delivered to American Airlines in February 1962, but was sold to the first of several subsequent owners just five years later. American originally ordered 25 990s, but ended up taking only 20 after performance problems were discovered. American bought 15 of the 20 on condition that they were guaranteed to cruise at 584 mph. A further five were taken on the proviso that Convair could modify the aircraft to cruise at 620 mph. In the meantime, they operated at the same speed as American's Boeing 707 and 720s, and were thus effectively lower capacity, fuel thirsty, versions of the two Boeings. American later sold all but one of its original 990s, the odd-one out having been destroyed by fire at Newark, New Jersey, in 1963

Above Convair CV-990s become familiar sights in Europe well into the 1980s thanks to Spantax, a Spanish charter operator, which operated a total of 14 second hand aircraft. Here, wingtip vortices stream from EC-BZO as it climbs up into the late afternoon sunlight over Devon on one of its final charter flights from Exeter in November of 1986. Originally delivered to American Airlines as N5618 in 1962, this CV-990 later flew for MEA. The Beirut-based carrier traded it back to American in October 1971 in return for a Boeing 720B and three months later the aircraft was sold to Spantax. In 1988 Spantax donated it to the Cuatro Vientos Museo del Aire Museum. A sister aircraft, EC-BJC, proved the strength of the basic CV-990 design when it survived a mid-air collision with an Iberia DC-9 during a French Air Traffic Controllers strike in 1973. The CV-990 lost 18 ft of one wing and landed safely, but the DC-9 crashed

CONVAIR CV-990

Type: medium-range passenger transport
Span: 36.58 m (120 ft)
Length: 42.43 m (139 ft 2½ in)
Height: 12.04 m (39 ft 6 in)
Wing area: 209 m² (2250 sq ft)
Weight: maximum 114,760 kg (253,000 lbs); empty 54,840 kg (120,900 lbs)
Powerplant: four 7280-kg (16,050-lb) st General Electric CJ-805-23C aft-fan turbofans
Performance: maximum cruising speed 990 km/h (615 mph); economical cruising speed 895 km/h (556 mph); range with maximum payload and reserves 6115 km (3800 miles)
Payload: 11,992 kg (26,440 lbs); seats for 149 passengers in service with Spantax
Crew: four
Production: 37

Right The jet that started it all. The revolutionary de Havilland Comet was the world's first jet airliner, and it first flew in July 1949. However, instead of giving Britain an unbeatable lead in commercial aviation it paid the ultimate price of being the pioneer. In 1954, two early Comet 1 aircraft, the third and eleventh off the Hatfield line, were lost to explosive decompressions at high altitude stemming from the previously unknown phenomena of metal fatigue. The Comet programme never really recovered from the blows, whilst at the same time vital lessons were learnt by Boeing and Douglas. One of the few Comets still in existence is preserved, ironically, at Boeing's Everett assembly site where 747, 767 and 777s are built. The Comet 4C is painted in BOAC livery, but was never actually used by the British airline. It first flew in 1959 and served Mexicana from 1960 to 1970 as XA-NAS 'Golden Aztec'. It passed through the hands of several owners before ending up in store at Paine Field, Everett, in January 1980. The aircraft is pictured under a rain-washed northwestern sky in the spring of 1989. A direct ancestor of the Comet, the British Aerospace Nimrod, is currently still in service with the Royal Air Force as an anti-submarine warfare and electronic reconnaisance aircraft

HAWKER SIDDELEY COMET 4

(data for Comet 4C)

Powerplant: four Rolls-Royce Avon RA29 Mk525B turbojet engines (each 10,500 lbs; 4763 kg st)

Wing span: 114 ft 10 in (35.00 m)

Length overall: 118 ft 0 in (35.97 m)

Cabin, excluding flight deck: length 79 ft 2 in (24.13 m); Max width 9 ft 7 in (2.92 m); Max height 6 ft 6½ in (2.00 m); Volume 3160 cu ft (89.5 m³)

Freight holds: rear 190 cu ft (5.38 m³) front underfloor 223 cu ft (6.32 m³) rear underfloor 246 cu ft (6.97 m³)

Capacity payload: 22,900 lbs (10,400 kg)

Max T-O weight: 162,000 lbs (73,500 kg)

Mean cruising speed: at 31,000 ft (9450 m), 471 kts (542 mph; 872 km/h)

Range: in still air, with reserves, with 19,630 lbs (8900 kg) payload, 2250 nm (2590 miles; 4168 km)

Accommodation: flight crew of four and seating for up to 101 passengers

Variants:

Comet 4: standard-span 'stretched' development of earlier Comet 1/2/3: 111 ft 6 in (33.98 m) fuselage, seating up to 97 passengers and Avon Mk 524 turbojets

Comet 4B: short-span (107 ft 10 in; 32.87 m), long-fuselage version (118 ft 0 in; 35.97 m), seating up to 101 passengers; Avon Mk 525B engines

Comet 4C: combines standard wing of Comet 4 with powerplant and long fuselage of Comet 4B: see data. Built also for RAF (5); two converted as Nimrod prototypes

Above Britain's Vickers VC10 was built around a BOAC requirement for a long range jet transport capable of operating non-stop to East Africa. To meet the additional demand for spritely take-off performance, Vickers placed four engines at the tail and kept the wing uncluttered for maximum use of high-lift devices. The result was a graceful design with a high cantilever T-tail and a large swept wing. The drawbacks included drag problems around the tail and a heavy wing structure to counteract the lack of bending relief that would have normally been available from wing-mounted engines. The type's excellent field performance, coupled with its long-range, made it a suitable transport for the Royal Air Force, which took 14 Model 1106s for Transport Command. One of these jets, XR808, is pictured overhead its base at RAF Brize Norton in Oxfordshire. The pronounced leading edge slats are clearly displayed. Two basic variants of VC10 were produced: Standard and Super. The RAF versions uniquely combined the Rolls-Royce Conway RCo.43 engines and tail fin fuel tank of the Super VC10 with the smaller overall airframe dimensions of the Standard Model 1102. This VC10, named 'Kenneth Campbell VC', was delivered to the RAF on 7 July 1966. It has subsequently become part of the largest VC10 fleet assembled as the RAF has bought up ex-British Airways (BOAC), Gulf Air and East African Airways Super and Standard models for conversion into tankers

---

VICKERS VC10

Type: long-range passenger/cargo transport
Span: (-1100) 42.72 m (140 ft 2 in); (-1101/-1109) 44.55 m (146 ft 2 in)
Length: 48.38 m (158 ft 8 in)
Height: 12.04 m (39 ft 6 in)
Wing area: (-1100/-1101) 264.9 m² (2851 sq ft); (-1102/-1109) 272.8 m² (2936 sq ft)
Weight: maximum (civil) 142,430 kg (314,000 lb); (-1109, RAF) 146,510 kg (323,000 lb); empty (typical) 66,670 kg (146,979 lb)
Powerplant: four Rolls-Royce Conway two-shaft turbofans, (civil) 9240-kg (20,370-lb) Conway 540s; (RAF) 9888-kg (21,800-lb) Conway 301s
Performance: maximum cruising speed 914 km/h (568 mph); economical cruising speed 886 km/h (550 mph); range with maximum payload and no reserves (civil) 8115 km (5040 miles); (RAF) 6275 km (3900 miles)
Payload: (civil, typical) 18,039 kg (39,769 lbs); (RAF) 26,030 kg (57,400 lbs); seats for up to 151 passengers
Crew: three to five
Production: 32

Above The VC10 was the last complete aircraft to be built and assembled at Weybridge, marking the end of a 50-year aircraft building tradition at Vickers. It is fitting, therefore, that a VC10 has been donated for preservation at the nearby Brooklands Museum. The aircraft, A40-AB, is a Model 1103 and first flew in October 1964. If was operated by British United Airways, later British Caledonian Airways, for 10 years before being bought by the Oman Government in 1974. It was donated to the museum in 1987

BAC SUPER VC10

Type: long-range passenger transport (-1154, passenger/cargo)
Span: 4.55 m (146 ft 2 in)
Length: 52.32 m (171 ft 8 in)
Height: 12.04 m (39 ft 6 in)
Wing area: 272.4 m² (2932 sq ft)
Weight: maximum 151,950 kg (335,000 lb); empty (-1151) 71,940 kg (158,594 lbs)
Powerplant: four 9888-kg (21,800-lb) st Rolls-Royce Conway 550 two-shaft turbofans
Performance: maximum cruising speed 935 km/h (581 mph); economical cruising speed 886 km/h (550 mph); range with maximum payload and no reserves 7600 km (4720 miles)
Payload: (-1151, passenger) 22,860 kg (50,406 lb); (-1154 passenger/cargo) 27,360 kg (60,321 lbs); seats for up to 187 passengers
Crew: three to five
Production: 22

Right Addressing the Royal Aeronautical Society in London in the enlightened Glasnost era, a designer from the Ilyushin bureau asked if his learned audience noticed any resemblance between the Il-62 and the VC10. 'Imitation is the sincerest form of flattery', is how he explained the genesis of the airliner which NATO codenamed *Classic*. The Il-62 formed the backbone of Aeroflot's long-haul services during the 1960s. Powered by four tail-mounted Kuznetsov NK-8-4 turbofans, the aircraft can carry up to 186 passengers over ranges of up to 4160 miles (6700 km) with full fuel load. A distinctive feature of the Il-62, and one which is virtually unheard of in western-built airliners, is the standard use of in-flight thrust reverser before landing. Thrust reversers on the outboard engines are deployed as the aircraft approaches the runway threshold to land and help shorten the resulting run. Improvements made to later models, dubbed Il-62M and MK, allow up to 195 passengers to be carried. Built in 1966, CCCP-86670 now resides at the Monino museum next to an Li-2 (Russian licence-built DC-3). Like the VC10, the Il-62's T-tail and rear mounted engines gave it some tight aft centre of gravity limits, particularly when on the ground. As a result, the designers fitted the aircraft with a hydraulic twin-wheel strut to support the rear fuselage during loading and unloading

ILYUSHIN Il-62

(data for Il-62M)

Powerplant: four Soloviev D-30KU turbofan engines (each 23,530 lbs; 11,500 kg st)

Wing span: 141 ft 9 in (43.20 m)

Length : 174 ft 3¼ in (53.12 m)

Cabin: Max width 11 ft 5½ in (3.49 m) Max height 6 ft 11½ in (2.12 m), Volume 5756 cu ft (163 m³)

Total volume of pressure cell: 13,985 cu ft (396 m³)

Cargo hold volume: underfloor (two, total) 1380 cu ft (39.1 m³) rear fuselage 205 cu ft (5.8 m³)

Max payload: 50,700 lbs (23,000 kg)

Max T-O weight: 363,760 lbs (165,000 kg)

Normal cruising speed: 458-486 kts (528-560 mph; 850-900 km/h)

Normal cruising height: 33,000 to 39,400 ft (10,000 to 12,000 m)

Range: with max payload, with reserves, 4315 nm (4970 miles; 8000 km)

Accommodation: flight crew of five and seating for up to 186 passengers. Forward underfloor baggage and freight hold accommodates nine containers, each weighing approxiately 100 lbs (45 kg) empty and with a capacity of 1322 lbs (600 kg) and 56.5 cu ft (1.6 m³). Rear hold accommodates five similar containers. Two compartments for non-containerised cargo

Variants:

Il-62: Original productionv version (up to 186 passengers), with 23,150 lb (10,500 kg) st Kuznetsov NK-8-4 turbofans

Il-62M: longer-range version (see data), with different engines, thrust reversers, additional fuel tank in fin, revised flight deck layout, containerised baggage and freight system, and other refinements

Il-62MK: Version of Il-62M with higher operating weights and seats for up to 195 passengers